Management for Professio

The Springer series *Management for Professionals* comprises high-level business and management books for executives. The authors are experienced business professionals and renowned professors who combine scientific background, best practice, and entrepreneurial vision to provide powerful insights into how to achieve business excellence.

More information about this series at http://www.springer.com/series/10101

Oliver Treidler

Transfer Pricing in One Lesson

A Practical Guide to Applying the Arm's Length Principle in Intercompany Transactions

Springer

Oliver Treidler
Berlin, Germany

Additional material to this book can be downloaded from http://extras.springer.com.

ISSN 2192-8096 ISSN 2192-810X (electronic)
Management for Professionals
ISBN 978-3-030-25087-4 ISBN 978-3-030-25085-0 (eBook)
https://doi.org/10.1007/978-3-030-25085-0

Cover design: eStudio Calamar, Berlin/Figueres

This Springer imprint is published by the registered company Springer Nature Switzerland AG.
The registered company address is: Gewerbestrasse 11, 6330 Cham, Switzerland

Foreword

Transfer Pricing in One Lesson, according to its author Oliver Treidler, is designed as a pragmatic survival kit—not a "magic bullet"—for handling the day-to-day challenges facing a transfer pricing (TP) professional. While the book is a practical guide aimed at young TP professionals working in consulting or industry who have been asked to apply the OECD's post-BEPS Transfer Pricing Guidelines, I suspect all TP professionals will find the book useful reading. I've been studying transfer pricing for 45 years and still find *Transfer Pricing in One Lesson* helpful reading, so I suspect others will also.

Treidler argues that to be successful as a TP professional one must understand the arm's length principle and how to apply it to specific situations. The book starts with "one key lesson" (the basics of transfer pricing), which is then applied to a variety of specific situations. To illustrate the cases and provide a real-world feel for the lesson, Treidler creates a fictitious multinational (MNE), the Prima Group, and explores how the lesson can be applied in different situations.

The core message in the book is that transfer pricing is an art, not a science, where "the art of transfer pricing consists in never losing sight of the reality of a specific business when applying the arm's length principle." Treidler recognizes that there are both business and tax considerations that affect transfer pricing choices, and he is mindful that the TP professional must find an "appropriate balance" between these pressures. To be successful at finding this appropriate balance, he argues that "you have to avoid the myopia of a fragmented transaction-by-transaction type of analysis and always be mindful of the economic essence of the business relationship as a whole."

To do this, the TP professional must align the firm's transfer pricing structure with the firm's business model. Treidler says, "the first and foremost task of a transfer pricing consultant is therefore to understand the business model of his client and ensure that the model is accurately translated into a tax viable transfer pricing structure."

Treidler argues that successful alignment depends on two tools or processes that can be used to translate the firm's business into an analytical framework that can be used for tax purposes. These two processes are:

- Establishing an adequate level of segmentation of the firm's transactions
- Performing a value chain analysis for each identified transaction or group of transactions

The first process—segmenting the business into transactions—builds on industry analyses such as Porter's five forces model to identify the "commercial relations" and the "conditions and economically relevant circumstances" between the related parties. Such identification, of course, is required as part of a comparability analysis under the OECD's Transfer Pricing Guidelines.

The second process, also required by the Transfer Pricing Guidelines, is value chain analysis (which he refers to as a functional and risk (F&R) analysis). Treidler views value chain analysis as the "heart and soul of transfer pricing." Each entity in the MNE group must be identified in a general way, based on its functional and risk profiles, as either a low-risk, low-return (routine) entity or a high-risk, high-return (entrepreneurial) entity. The routine entity should receive a routine (arm's length) return in line with its routine functions and risks. The appropriate amount can be determined by treating the routine entity as the tested party and using a one-sided transfer pricing method to determine its arm's length return. The entrepreneurial entity is then compensated with the residual return after the routine entity or entities have received their return.

The functional and risk analysis forces the TP professional to "dissect the business model of the MNE." With that model, the TP professional can identify which entity should be the tested party and come to a high-level understanding of what an arm's length allocation of profits should be to that entity. Treidler argues that amount should intuitively be appropriate from both business and tax perspectives.

With the basic lesson in place, Treidler then moves to applying the lesson to the types of transactions that are likely to face a young TP professional. Each situation is illustrated with the Prima Group case. As one might expect, he starts with CUP, the comparable uncontrolled price, and then moves through the basic methods. I summarize some of the insights here:

- CUP: Comparing "Like with like" is not a trivial task.
- Resale Price Method: Comparability doesn't stop at the gross margin.
- TNMM: Arm's length net margins should make everyone happy.
- Profit Split Method: Internal negotiations are useful for approximating an arm's length allocation of profits within the MNE provided that entities engage in real negotiations.
- (Net) Cost Plus Method: Arm's length net margins should make everyone happy.

The book goes on to apply the lesson to more complex transactions, in particular to transfer pricing of management services and financial transactions. Lastly, Treidler discusses the critical importance of properly prepared documentation for the tax authorities.

Three annexes end the book. They are: (1) a Transfer Pricing Basics Questionnaire, (2) a Checklist for Benchmarking Studies, and (3) an Application of a CUP License Fee. In addition, three Excel-based tools are available in a supplementary online package: (1) Value Chain Analysis Tool, (2) Cost Allocation Tool, and (3) Cash Pool Tool. TP professionals, especially those new to the field, will find the annexes very helpful.

Treidler has several years of experience as a transfer pricing practitioner, first for Big Four firms and later in his own consulting practice where he also offers workshops on transfer pricing and value chain analysis. The book is written in a practical and captivating style—as if the author were talking directly to the reader—which should give it a broad appeal, not only to beginning TP professionals but to those who are further along in their careers also.

It's clear from reading this book that the author is passionate about transfer pricing. He believes—as do I—that the arm's length standard is the best way to value related party transactions within the MNE group, best not only for tax purposes but also because—when properly done—the arm's length standard best captures the realities of the MNE's activities.

Can transfer pricing be taught in one lesson? I believe that yes it can—and Treidler shows us how it can be done. I enjoyed reading this book and believe you will do so also. Enjoy!

Texas A&M University, TX, USA Lorraine Eden
May 5, 2019

Contents

About the Author

Oliver Treidler is CEO and founder of TP&C GmbH based in Berlin. TP&C is an independent provider of consulting services, including sub-contracting services, for projects focused on transfer pricing and controlling. The consulting philosophy of TP&C, which is also the leitmotiv of *Transfer Pricing in One Lesson*, is deeply rooted in a business perspective on transfer pricing—i.e., "talking business not legalese."

Prior to founding TP&C, Oliver worked as a senior manager in the transfer pricing department of a top 10 auditing and consulting firm in Berlin. He learned the ropes of transfer pricing while working for two of the Big Four in Frankfurt and Hamburg.

Oliver frequently publishes on transfer pricing issues and actively contributed to various public discussion procedures of the OECD BEPS project. He holds a master's degree in international economics and European studies from the Corvinus University of Budapest (M.Sc.) and a Ph.D. in economics from the University of Würzburg.

Contact Information:
ot@tp and c.de
www.tp-and-c.de

Chapter 1
Introduction

The title of the book is intended as a homage to Henry Hazlitt, whose timeless masterpiece "*Economics in One Lesson*" has been such a wonderful and inspirational book to many economists—at least those sympathizing with the Austrian School of economics.

This book on transfer pricing contains a healthy dose of economics as well as general aspects from the field of international business. Like Hazlitt's book, *Transfer Pricing in One Lesson* is primarily written for the "beginner" in this highly specialized field, including students interested in subjects such as law, economics, business, or politics. Most importantly, I hope that (young) transfer pricing practitioners and employees in tax or accounting departments will find helpful guidance in this book. I am relentless in teaching the lessons to my own employees and my intention is twofold; first, I want to provide them with a frame of reference that will be useful throughout their future careers as transfer pricing consultants; second, I want them to enjoy transfer pricing.

While working and learning during actual projects is always good, it is sometimes hard for young professionals to see the "big picture"; i.e., when your first assignment is to participate in a complex project focused on analyzing a cash pool of a large MNE and your second assignment is to contribute on a loan benchmark for another large MNE, chances are that you will have a hard time to take a breath and think about the nature and beauty of the profession you have (presumably) stumbled into. Well, take a breath (drink some coffee) and take some time to learn about the basics of transfer pricing; i.e., learn about the arm's length principle. My advice to you is: spend time on the basics early in your career; you will have to specialize soon enough. This book should allow you to learn in your own time and at your own speed (will not show up on your time card) and you may even want to use it as a conversation starter with one of your more experienced colleagues.

Just as reading Ludwig van Mises's "*Human Action*," regardless of the unquestioned greatness of the book, is likely to be "overkill" for those beginning to grapple with the subject of economics, the transfer pricing tomes written by leading figures in the field such as Alexander Vögele as well as the countless

O. Treidler, *Transfer Pricing in One Lesson*, Management for Professionals,
https://doi.org/10.1007/978-3-030-25085-0_1

OECD Publications are simply overwhelming for those with a professional life outside of transfer pricing. Thus, the structure of this book is designed to provide the reader with **one key lesson** and to subsequently apply this lesson to a host of specific examples. The examples will be provided within "case study" subsections, which will introduce you to a fictitious MNE, the "Prima Group," navigating through day-to-day transfer pricing challenges that may be familiar to you. The aim is to equip you with a pragmatic "survival kit" for your day-to-day transfer pricing challenges. In other words, this book is not designed to mutate into some sort of "chic" reference that can be cited in tax memos but rather intended to serve you as a guidebook—helping you never to lose your orientation, even when confronted with more intricate transfer pricing issues.

The core message of *Economics in One Lessons* can be summarized as

> the art of economics consists in looking not merely at the immediate but at the longer effects of any act or policy; it consists in tracing the consequences of that policy not merely for one group but for all groups (H. Hazlitt)

The core message of *Transfer Pricing in One Lesson* can suitably be summarized as ***the art of transfer pricing consists in never losing sight of the reality of a specific business when applying the arm's length principle; to find an appropriate balance between the business and the tax considerations, you have to avoid the myopia of a fragmented transaction-by-transaction type of analysis and instead always be mindful of the economic essence of the business relationship as a whole***.

Somewhat opposed to Hazlitt, I do not intend to focus on unmasking fallacies in the economic reasoning of others but rather provide the reader with references to expertise from people who I have encountered in my professional life as a transfer pricing consultant and to whom, in my opinion, it is worthwhile to listen. I have tried to write this book as simply and with as much freedom from technicalities as is consistent with reasonable accuracy. Due to the opacity of the subject, this book can be no more than a starting point for your further studies and I sincerely hope that it may motivate you to embark on that journey.

Lastly, I am painfully aware that many employees in tax or accounting departments that are being forced to cope with transfer pricing regard this assignment as either boring or dreadful, especially when dealing with tax lawyers or tax advisors, who, not entirely without cause, are prone to emphasize the myriad of risks involved in transfer pricing. Well, again, this book is designed as a "survival kit" (not a magic bullet). Gaining an improved understanding of the arm's length principle will bring you a long way toward minimizing transfer pricing-related tax risks (not eliminating them). To effectively cope with transfer pricing challenges, think about business and economics first and about tax law second. To achieve a sustainable transfer pricing system, it is much more important to have a solid understanding about your business than to have expert knowledge of idiosyncratic laws and regulations. This is especially true, as transfer pricing practitioners will have to cope with a truckload of differing national regulations, while the definition of the arm's length principle is luckily (largely) the same around the globe.

So, in other words, borrowed from another beloved Guidebook, "*Don't Panic*."

Chapter 2
The Lesson

To successfully deal with transfer pricing issues, you will have to understand the arm's length principle and learn how to apply it to your specific situation. It is that simple—at least for as long as all nations continue to fundamentally base their regulations on the arm's length paradigm. Because each individual group member of an MNE is subject to tax on the income arising to it (so-called "separate entity approach"),[1] the attention of tax authorities is naturally focused on the nature of the transactions between these individual members and on whether the conditions thereof differ from the conditions that would be obtained in comparable uncontrolled transactions. Such an analysis of the controlled and uncontrolled transactions, which is referred to as a "comparability analysis," is at the heart of the application of the arm's length principle.[2]

Now, what is the essence of the arm's length principle? Well, pursuant to the arm's length principle, MNEs are required to price their intercompany transactions by utilizing prices that are (or would be) agreed between unrelated third parties in comparable circumstances. By basing the pricing of intercompany transactions on such a reference, i.e., (hypothetical) market prices, the artificial shifting of profits between companies of MNE located in different jurisdictions ought to be prevented. Again, this sounds rather straightforward but not quite so fast.

It is often not easy to identify market prices that can be used as an appropriate reference. Thinking about how complex the issue of "value and pricing" is and seeing how these concepts evolved throughout history, i.e., from the "labor theory of value" to the "subjective-utility value theory," it should hardly be a surprising statement that "there is no one 'true', 'correct' or 'universal' price for a good or a

[1]See OECD (2017a), Paragraph, 1.5. **Note**: These Guidelines will be quoted frequently throughout this book—so all OECD references (i.e., "OECD Guidelines" or "OECD-GL") will refer to these Guidelines unless indicated otherwise. The OECD-GL are arguably the main international reference for transfer pricing—reading this book will ensure that you are familiar with the most important provisions contained in the OECD-GL.

[2]See OECD Guidelines (2017a), Paragraph, 1.6.

O. Treidler, *Transfer Pricing in One Lesson*, Management for Professionals,
https://doi.org/10.1007/978-3-030-25085-0_2

service". Hence, even without further addressing pricing theory at this point,[3] the notion of a "natural uncertainty" of a specific price seems hardly controversial. The price agreed between two contracting parties will always depend on the specific circumstances of the transaction, i.e., considering factors such as the volume, the timing, and the prevailing market conditions.

Does the fact that pricing is a complex issue render the arm's length principle to be an "unworkable concept"? Well, I do not think so—therefore, I am bothering to write this book. The key point worth emphasizing here is that one should not clamor to misguided notions such as the "correct" or "true" price. Even in third-party transactions, a price list is usually not applied universally to all customers, as there will almost always be room to negotiate. Opposed to market transactions, intercompany transactions are, at least most of the time,[4] characterized by a lower degree of negotiation between the transacting parties (entities). That does not imply, however, that all (or even the majority of) MNEs have an automatic incentive to set their transfer prices in a way to minimize their overall tax bill. For MNEs (transfer) prices are of high importance in terms of being "market signals" for the efficient distribution of resources, i.e., to align incentives for the management with the objective of increasing the overall group profit. Distorting these signals is not necessarily the first thing that comes to mind. Yes, there are the Starbucks and Google out there, and we will discuss them in due course, but in general terms, there is no immediate reason why MNEs would purposefully misalign their transfer pricing from their business processes. In this context, the OECD correctly points out, and it is certainly worthwhile to remind some of the more overzealous tax auditors, that "Tax administrations should not automatically assume that associated enterprises have sought to manipulate their profits. There may be a genuine difficulty in accurately determining a market price in the absence of market forces or when adopting a particular commercial strategy."[5]

While identifying sufficiently comparable third-party transactions is one of the main challenges for transfer pricing professionals, it can always be achieved thanks to the flexibility of the arm's length principle. Also, it will most often be feasible to align market signals and the transfer pricing system applied for intercompany transactions. As a sensible starting point, one should embrace the concept that "transfer pricing is not an exact science"[6] (quoting the OECD's equivalent of the concept that there is no one "true" price). Consequently, transfer prices are often set by MNEs within a (broad) range of "comparable" arm's length prices. From an entrepreneurial point of view, this is sensible. A range of prices reflects differences in terms of market conditions, bargaining positions, and other phenomena prevailing in a market economy. As such, utilizing a range of prices as a reference for transfer pricing rather

[3]For an entertaining introduction (on the water-diamond paradox), I highly recommend the essay by Sanchez (2011).

[4]Note: Make no mistake—infighting among individual profit centers within an MNE can be fierce.

[5]See OECD-GL (2017a), Paragraph 1.2.

[6]OECD-GL (2017a), Paragraph 1.13.

than a single price is hardly an artificial or sinister approach concocted by tax advisors. Entrepreneurs will often utilize a certain range in order to further their strategic objectives, e.g., ensuring a sensible incentive structure for distribution entities.

Critics of the arm's length principle tend to lament that MNEs systematically abuse transfer pricing by setting transfer prices that favor subsidiaries located in low tax countries. The criticism is, however, largely misguided, as setting transfer prices within a range of reference prices seldom offers an enticing "lever" to shift profits.[7] It should also be noted that tax authorities are notoriously suspicious of benchmark studies, which are utilized by taxpayers to determine and defend arm's length ranges, and do not hesitate to attack respective studies. In other words, it is plainly implausible to portray transfer pricing as a main pressure point of tax avoidance (let alone tax evasion[8]). It is largely uncontested that aggressive tax avoidance schemes are based on legal elements and elaborate tax structuring, such as hybrid mismatches, etc., rather than on systematic mispricing. By embracing and propagating the entrepreneurial perspective on transfer pricing, academics as well as the business community might succeed in countering the stigmatization of transfer pricing as a vehicle for tax avoidance. A respective shift in the perception of transfer pricing will be vital for preserving the arm's length principle as the globally accepted paradigm of transfer pricing. Should the arm's length principle continue to be publicly discredited, there is a real possibility of formulary apportionment unseating the arm's length principle as the leading paradigm. In a nutshell, this would imply that profits would be allocated among the entities of a MNE pursuant to an arbitrary ("politically agreed") formula based on allocation factors derived from the balance sheet of the MNE. In other words, any link between the market prices or business processes and transfer pricing would be cut off.[9]

Returning to the one lesson of transfer pricing, it must be emphasized that the art of transfer pricing consists in never losing sight of the reality of a specific business when applying the arm's length principle. You have to avoid the myopia of a fragmented transaction-by-transaction type of analysis and always be mindful of the economic essence of the business relationship as a whole. One of the cardinal sins of transfer pricing is to overlook the forest in a precise and minute examination of individual trees.

---

[7]Note: As will be discussed below, the lever is much smaller when adopting profit margins of comparable companies as references (i.e. when applying Cost Plus of TNMM)—this form of benchmarking is by far the most frequently utilized reference in day-to-day transfer pricing.

[8]In this context, the OECD also is correct in pointing out that "*The consideration of transfer pricing should not be confused with the consideration of problems of tax fraud or tax avoidance, even though transfer pricing policies may be used for such purposes*"—see OECD-GL (2017a), Paragraph 1.2. For a quick but witty insight on this issue, I recommend reading Forstater (2018).

[9]For a brief account on the importance of an entrepreneurial approach to transfer pricing to counter, the momentum gained by the proponents of formulary apportionment, please refer to Treidler (2017).

But how can you ensure that you adequately align your transfer pricing structure with your business model? Well, as a starting point, it essentially boils down to applying the following two "tools" or "processes":

(a) Establishing an adequate level of segmentation (aggregation) for your transactions
(b) Conducting a value chain analysis for each of the identified transactions

When appropriately applied, these tools provide you with an efficient "translation" of your business into analytical framework that can be utilized for tax purposes. Both tools are indispensable for applying the arm's length principle and cannot be substituted. Neglecting to pay proper attention to dealing with these basics will result in an inherently flawed transfer pricing system and unavoidably lead to "systemic" transfer pricing risks. So, let us take the time to take a closer look at both tools in the following subsections.

2.1 Developing a Broad Understanding of the Relevant Economic Conditions for Your Transactions

A keen understanding of the industry and the relevant economic circumstances (as defined in Fig. 2.1) is vital for each company—not just for tax or transfer pricing but, more importantly, for having commercial success. To gather the facts and figures that are relevant for transfer pricing, the practitioner (the in-house specialist as well as an external consultant) needs to tap into the (readily) available know-how. It will pay dividends to talk to the respective people and always try to gain a balanced perspective by talking to people from different divisions and business units. One of the most intriguing and rewarding aspects of working in transfer pricing is the opportunity to talk to different entrepreneurs and to learn about a wide variety of business models. Most of them tend to be enthusiastic and willing to explain, i.e., they need very little prompting and you really do not have to be an expert in any specific industry to understand the basic parameters of the business model—there is

OECD Guidelines 2017, Paragraph 1.33 and 1.34

Application of the arm's length principle is based on a comparison of the conditions in a controlled transaction with the conditions that would have been made had the parties been independent and undertaking a comparable transaction under comparable circumstances.

1. Identify the commercial relations between the associated enterprises and the conditions and economically relevant circumstances attaching to those relations in order that the controlled transaction is accurately delineated;
2. The typical process of identifying the commercial relations between the associated enterprises and the conditions and economically relevant circumstances attaching to those relations requires a broad-based understanding of the industry sector in which the MNE group operates and of the factors affecting the performance of any business operating in that sector.

Fig. 2.1 Defining a broad-based understanding of relevant economic conditions (source: OECD)

virtually no need for compiling tedious questionnaires; you can instead focus on addressing the key-questions (see below).[10] In other words, listen and be unbiased, i.e., do not fence-in the narrative by introducing transfer pricing-specific concepts such as "low value-added services" at the early stages of an interview.

Sometimes the analytical process described above is termed "industrial analysis." While this is certainly a sensible term, it can be a little misleading in terms of the required scope of the analysis. When we are talking about an MNE that is to be considered a global player (as a rule of thumb it seems appropriate to adopt the country-by-country reporting threshold of revenues exceeding 750 €. EUR for identifying "global players"), you should devote substantial time (and budget) to perform a rather detailed analysis. Looking at the "value creation analysis" (VCA) championed by Michael Porter provides you with a solid analytical framework.[11] The industrial analysis should be focused on evaluating "(Porters) five forces," i.e.:

1. Bargaining power of suppliers
2. Threat of new entrants
3. Bargaining power of buyers
4. Threat of substitute products or services
5. Rivalry among existing competitors (firms)

Now, when we are talking about smaller MNEs, you should not hesitate to resort to a high-level analysis instead. At the end of the day, you will have to be able to answer the following key question:

- What are the key success factors for the MNE in the specific (segment of the) industry?[12]

Additional questions should focus on the specificities regarding the acquisition process as well as the pricing structure.

For documentation purposes, the bulk of the required information can directly be derived from the annual reports of the MNE. When compiling a transfer pricing documentation, the industrial analysis should be integrated into the Master File (see OECD Guidelines 2017a, paragraph 1.34) as it pertains to the entire group and does not address individual entities.

Conducting a broad-based analysis of the taxpayers' circumstances constitutes a first step in a comparability analysis, by ensuring that the relevant economic

---

[10]Just to be on the safe side, you will find a concise (10-point) questionnaire in the Annex A. The issues discussed in Chap. 2 of this book are essentially covered by questions 1–3.

[11]Please note that this is a highly abbreviated description of a VCA. For guidance on applying a full-scope VCA for transfer pricing purposes, I recommend Baumgartner (2018).

[12]Complementary or refining questions would be: What is the competitive advantage of the company? What is the competitive strategy of the company? See also Baumgartner (2018), who defines "competitive strategy" as "choosing a different set of activities to deliver a unique mix of value. Competitive strategy is the search for a favorable competitive position in an industry, the fundamental arena in which competition occurs".

conditions are adequately considered—without (yet) looking at specific transactions.[13] As emphasized by the OECD in Section A.3 of Chapter III. within the OECD Guidelines 2017a; *"Ideally, in order to arrive at the most precise approximation of arm's length conditions, the arm's length principle should be applied on a transaction-by-transaction basis*". Thus, building upon the broad-based understanding of the business model and the relevant economic circumstances, you will have to determine an appropriate level of segmentation for your transactions. In day-to-day practice, following a transaction-by-transaction approach will translate into the necessity of having to conduct multiple analyses and greatly drive-up the administrative burden. The question that you must confront prior to commencing with a comparability analysis is thus: "Given the specific features of my business model, will a transaction-by-transaction analysis be the most suitable approach to approximate arm's length conditions?".

The OECD emphasizes that "[...] there are often situations where separate transactions are so closely linked or continuous that they cannot be evaluated adequately on a separate basis" and provides rather useful guidance for answering the question formulated above (see OECD Guidelines 2017a, paragraph 3.9) listing the following examples:

- Long-term contracts for the supply of commodities or services
- Rights to use intangible property[14]
- Pricing a range of closely linked products (e.g., in a product line) when it is impractical to determine pricing for each individual product or transaction
- Portfolio approaches, i.e., when following a business strategy consisting of bundling certain transactions for earning an appropriate return across the portfolio rather than necessarily on any single product within the portfolio.[15]

Aggregating transactions for conducting a comparability analysis will make your life easier, i.e., most importantly, you will not have to compile segmented or adjusted profit and loss accounting.[16] Hence, **devoting your time to assessing whether aggregating separate transactions is feasible will pay substantial dividends**. It would, however, be a mistake to cut corners at this stage. You need to provide an appropriate rationale for your decision to pursue an aggregated approach. Any such

[13]See OECD Guidelines (2017a), Paragraph 3.7.

[14]Note: The issues of intangibles will be addressed in detail in a separate section of this book (see below). For introductory purposes, it is sufficient to point out that the OECD here refers to the fact that intangibles are often transferred as a part of a "package"; i.e., "licensing of manufacturing know-how and the supply of vital components to an associated manufacturer; it may be more reasonable to assess the arm's length terms for the two items together rather than individually."

[15]Note: Popular examples for portfolio approaches include selling a package of technical equipment and the related captive aftermarket consumables (i.e., coffee machines and coffee capsules, or printers and cartridges)—See OECD Guidelines (2017a), Paragraph 3.7.

[16]See OECD Guidelines (2017a), Paragraphs 2.84 and 2.85, i.e., "Costs and revenues that are not related to the controlled transaction under review should be excluded where they materially affect comparability with uncontrolled transactions."

rationalization will have to be anchored in the broad-based analysis of the economic circumstances. Neglecting to appropriately document the rationale underlying the aggregation will expose you to systemic transfer pricing risk, i.e., a tax authority successfully challenging the aggregated approach will often be in a position to impose transfer pricings adjustments on a transaction-by-transaction basis. The respective guidance provided by the OECD, and the equivalent stipulations in national regulations,[17] should thus be taken seriously, i.e., *"portfolio approaches must be reasonably targeted as they should not be used to apply a transfer pricing method at the taxpayer's company-wide level in those cases where different transactions have different economic logic and should be segmented"* (see OECD Guidelines 2017a, paragraph 3.10).

Case Study: Meet the "Prima Group"

To apply the lesson to specific, real-life, examples, we will introduce the fictitious "Prima Group."[18] The main characteristics of the Prima Group can be summarized as follows:

- The Prima Group operates in the household electronics industry and is focused on developing innovative technologies for the home entertainment of the future.
- The organizational structure exhibits a comparatively high degree of centralization, with Prima GmbH, from its headquarters in Berlin, determining the business strategy and centrally monitoring the performance of all companies within the Prima Group. Also, all development, production, and marketing activities are controlled from Germany.
- The business activities of the foreign subsidiaries of Prima GmbH are mostly comprised of rendering sales support to Prima GmbH in their respective local markets. Depending on the requirements of the local markets (specific clients), the foreign subsidiaries can either act as resellers (i.e., subsidiaries contracting and invoicing directly with the local customer) or as commissionaires (i.e., contracting and invoicing are performed by Prima GmbH).
- It is the strategic goal of Prima to establish itself as a globally recognized technology leader. The Prima USP "premium home entertainment for everyone" stands for delivering value to customers by combining innovative technologies and competitive pricing.
- The home market (Germany) remains by far the dominant market for Prima. Some of the foreign subsidiaries are still in a start-up phase.

[17]Note: The relevant German Transfer Pricing Regulations (Verwaltungsgrundsätze—Verfahren, BMF-Schreiben v. 12.4.2015 ("Administrative Principles—Procedure") (Paragraph 3.4.13) are almost identical to the guidelines contained in the OECD Guidelines (which are explicitly referenced in this context).

[18]The Prima Group is entirely fictitious. As the OECD sometimes refers to the "Prima Group" in its examples, it seems appropriate to adopt the name—especially, as some aspects of the case studies will be based on OECD examples. Please note the disclaimer that we are dealing with somewhat simplified situations.

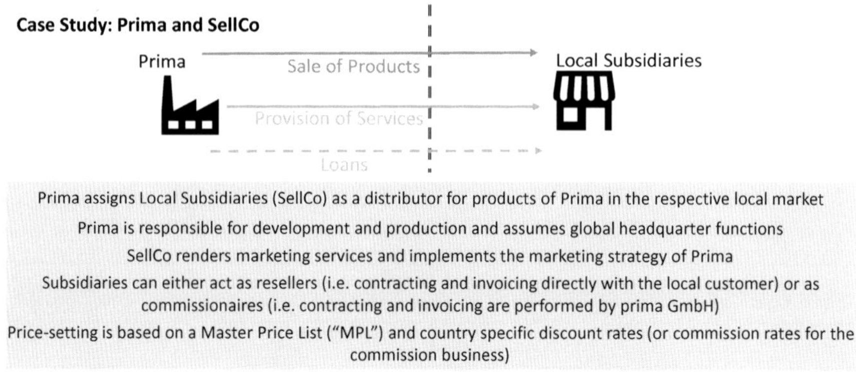

Fig. 2.2 Prima case study—main parameters (source: own illustration)

As you can see, the initial group structure is rather straightforward—but, be careful, you will see that the ostensible lack of complexity may be deceptive. To the more advanced practitioners, do not worry, we will add more complexity in later chapters.

The following intercompany transactions are conducted between Prima GmbH and the foreign subsidiaries:

(a) *Sale of Products* => Prima GmbH (Seller) has concluded "Cooperation and Sales Agreements" with the Local Entities (Buyer). The Agreements stipulate the rights and obligations of the parties, including the calculation of the compensation for the Buyer as a compensation for their local sales and support services. The price-setting is based on a Master Price List ("MPL") and country-specific discount rates (or commission rates for the Commission business).
(b) *Provision of Services* => Prima GmbH (Service Provider) has concluded "Service Agreements" with the Local Entities (Service Recipient). The Services are rendered by qualified personnel of Prima GmbH (administrative staff, IT specialists, and the Marketing and Management team). The Service Fee charged to the Local Entities is calculated by applying the Cost-Plus Method (C+).
(c) *Financial Transactions* => Prima (Lender) has granted loans to Local Entities (Borrower), applying the Comparable Uncontrolled Price (CUP) Method.

Figure 2.2 summarizes the main parameters of the case[19]:

[19]Note: As in many other disciplines, the use of illustrations can be highly advantageous also in transfer pricing. Most notably, it allows you emphasize the most important aspects of your transfer pricing system, while clarifying that certain other aspects are of subordinary nature. Among others, a consistent narrative will be important when deciding (arguing) on the aggregation of individual transactions and the limitation of the scope of a transfer pricing documentation (as will be demonstrated below).

Considering that the organizational setup of the Prima Group is rather centralized and straightforward, we can resort to a high-level analysis and focus on addressing the key question:

- What are the key success factors for the MNE in the specific (segment of the) industry?

Based on the facts and circumstances described above, it is reasonable to assume that the main drivers of the business profit (i.e., for delivering the USP) are the product development function and a high quality of the products as well as efficient manufacturing process. These functions need to be complemented by a coherent communications and marketing strategy.[20]

In the subsequent section, we will focus on delineating the value-added contribution by the transacting parties (i.e., Prima GmbH and the local subsidiaries) by conducting a functional and risk analysis. The functional and risk analysis will also yield additional insights with respect to the appropriate level of segmentation. Specifically, it will have to be evaluated whether an aggregation of the *sale of products* and the *provision of services* can be rationalized as being appropriate for the comparability analysis. Including the insights derived from the functional and risk analysis will greatly enhance the reliability of the rationalization of an aggregated approach.[21]

2.2 Functional and Risk Analysis: Heart and Soul of Transfer Pricing

The importance of the functional and risk analysis cannot be overestimated. As will be shown below, it constitutes the basis on which to select an appropriate transfer pricing method and will be the single most important point of reference when conducting a comparability analysis. The notion that the functions performed by an individual entity will determine its compensation (or profit potential) must be seen as the single most important guiding principle of applying the arm's length principle (see OECD Guidelines 2017a, Paragraph 1.51, as summarized in Fig. 2.3). Everything that follows are technical details (almost literally) of applying this guiding principle.

Having established a broad-based understanding of the key success factors for a specific MNE (see Sect. 2.1), the functional and risk analysis is focused on

[20]It is recommended that you utilize graphical illustrations to summarize and visualize the value chain of an MNE. A respective illustration can help you to sustain a coherent framework when quantifying the value of individual functions—I recommend the book by Osterwalder and Pigneur (2010) for pragmatic guidance and step-by-step guidance on how to use the so-called "business canvas" to illustrate your value chain.

[21]Note: In day-to-day transfer pricing practice, you should thus always defer the decision on the level of segmentation until the functional and risk analysis is concluded.

OECD Guidelines 2017, Paragraph 1.51

In transactions between two independent enterprises, **compensation usually will reflect the functions that each enterprise performs** (taking into account assets used and risks assumed).

The analysis focuses on **what the parties actually do** and the capabilities they provide. In particular, it is important to **understand how value is generated** by the group as a whole, the interdependencies of the functions performed by the associated enterprises with the rest of the group, and **the contribution that the associated enterprises make to that value creation.**

While one party may provide a large number of functions relative to that of the other party to the transaction, **it is the economic significance of those functions** in terms of their frequency, nature, and value to the respective parties to the transactions **that is important.**

Fig. 2.3 Focus on functions performed by transacting parties when applying the arm's length principle (source: OECD)

delineating the value contributions of individual entities, and as such, the functional and risk analysis can be understood as synonymous with a value chain analysis.[22] A functional and risk analysis will cut to the heart of the business model. The quality (tax viability) of the analysis will depend on efficiently translating the business-unit-oriented management perspective on the value-chain to a tax perspective based on the separate entity approach.[23] Some of the more important questions to discuss include:

- What functions are crucial for delivering the USP (i.e., delineate "core functions" from "support functions")?
- Which entities perform core functions, including high value-added functions related to unique and valuable intangibles?
- Which entities contribute supporting (routine) services that contribute merely low value-added?
- Is it feasible to quantify the value-added contributions of specific functions?

Addressing and answering these questions will generate a clear-cut picture of your business, which can be utilized in your internal and external communications and constitute the cornerstone of your transfer pricing system.

The analytical focus may often intuitively gravitate to the "functions" rather than the risks. One may argue that this does not constitute a severe problem in day-to-day practice, some cautionary remarks, however, must be made at this point. The revisions to the OECD Guidelines induced by the BEPS feature an enhanced focus on evaluating risks. This is highlighted, among others, by the strict provisions

[22]Yes, arguments could be made that a value chain analysis is generally more comprehensive than a functional and risk analysis, but for practical purposes, this is a rather moot point.

[23]These two differing perspectives tend to have a rather substantial impact on day-to-day transfer pricing. One of the central arguments to be derived from the lesson is that a transfer pricing system that is based on (closely aligned to) the business realities will minimize respective conflicts and risks. For a concise explanation of the merits of such an "entrepreneurial approach" to transfer pricing, please refer to Treidler (2017).

contained in Section D.1.2.1 of the OECD Guidelines 2017a, specifically that "A functional analysis is incomplete unless the material risks assumed by each party have been identified and considered since the actual assumption of risks would influence the prices and other conditions of transactions between the associated enterprises" (see Paragraph 1.56). The reason for the enhanced emphasis on risk assumption must be seen in the fact that many of the aggressive tax avoidance schemes against which BEPS was targeted were based on assigning risks (and corresponding profits) to entities with insufficient economic substance, i.e., entities lacking the capability (know-how, discretionary authority or capitalization) to make the business decisions pertaining to the relevant risks. In such cases, the risks were artificially separated from the economic functions. The OECD correctly highlights that "[...] ***Identifying risks goes hand in hand with identifying functions and assets*** *and is integral to the process of identifying the commercial [...] relations between the associated enterprises [...]. The assumption of risks associated with a commercial opportunity affects the profit potential of that opportunity in the open market, and the allocation of risks assumed between the parties to the arrangement affects how profits or losses resulting from the transaction are allocated at arm's length through the pricing of the transaction*" *(see OECD Guidelines, Paragraph 1.57 and 1.58).*

Adequately considering risks is thus an integral part of applying the arm's length principle. In day-to-day transfer pricing practices, however, you will often find yourself dealing with a commercial situation in which you are alleviated from performing a separate and comprehensive risk analysis, i.e., in situations where the performance of functions and the assumption of corresponding risks are "naturally aligned" within the transfer pricing system.

It is often emphasized that transfer pricing is not an "exact science"—see OECD Guidelines 2017a, paragraphs 1.13, 3.55, and 4.8—and that the application of the arm's length principle requires the exercise of judgment on the part of both the tax administration and taxpayer. This notion, as we will see in the remainder of this book, is certainly true. As any transfer pricing professional will tell you, tax audits relating for transfer pricing often resemble a "bazaar" especially when it comes to discussing the issue of "comparability" and applicable arm's length range (see below). One piece of advice you should take to heart, however, is that a good functional and risk analysis will reduce transfer pricing related risks by about 75%.[24] In other words, you should focus on deriving a classification of the transacting parties from the functional and risk analysis that is as "ironclad" as possible. A robust functional and risk analysis will ensure that the choice of the

[24]Note: There is no empirical basis for this claim—which would be incredibly difficult to obtain, i.e., how would you collect data on transfer pricing tax adjustments that is sufficiently detailed to segment the adjustment according to different causes? It is, however, firmly rooted in experiences from tax audit proceeding (including my own as well as those of trusted colleagues) and will also be made plausible in the context of our Prima case study (see below). How accurate 75% is as an estimate is not that decisive, i.e., if you think 60% or 90% is closer to the truth, the message stays the same: "Focusing your efforts on the functional and risk analysis will pay dividends."

tested party and thus the general allocation of the residual profit cannot be effectively challenged by the authority. This is exactly the starting position you want to be in before entering the bazaar. Consequently, you should not shy away from allocating a substantial share of your resources to getting the functional and risk analysis right.

Paradoxically, coping with the remaining challenges, notably preparing a tax viable comparability analysis, is often much more expensive than a functional and risk analysis. While respective costs are sometimes unavoidable and still reflect a positive tradeoff,[25] you should always be mindful of the fact that the comparability analysis is ultimately based on the functional and risk analysis and will only be as solid as its foundation.

Case Study: Functional and Risk Analysis for the "Prima Group"

In the following, you are provided with a concise description of the main functions and risks assumed by Prima and its foreign subsidiaries in the context of their business relations.[26] The level of detail will always depend on the complexity of the business relationship under review. While it is thus difficult to provide generalized guidance on this matter, you can use the following "orientation": First, the significance of the individual stages of the value chain (main and secondary processes) for the total value added need to be highlighted, and second, the relative contributions between the parties to the stages must be delineated as clearly as possible. Again, it is strongly encouraged to utilize illustrations to save time and add clarity (see the illustration of the "functional profile [Fig. 2.4]"[27]).

For many tax practitioners, it is highly challenging to settle on a specific analytic approach. To provide you with detailed guidance on this crucial aspect, we have integrated our "TP&C Value Chain Analysis" Tool into this book (Excel tool is available for download). This will provide you with step-by-step guidance on conducting a value chain (functional and risk) analysis, including the determination of tax viable quantifications of value-added contributions, which we will also discuss in the advanced section (when applying the profit split method). For now, let us focus on the task at hand and derive an unambiguous classification for our Prima Group.

Prior to addressing individual functions, it is advantageous to re-state the insights derived from the industrial analysis and to add some general comments on how these insights will translate to the functional and risk analysis. In the case of the Prima Group, it was established that the USP of the Group is to provide "premium home

[25]Note: Make no mistake, even if, thanks to a good functional and risk analysis, only 25% of the potential risks are subjected to bazaar-type of negotiations with tax authorities, a good comparability analysis (benchmark) will often put you in a much-improved negotiation position. Depending on the monetary value of 25% of the risk potential, the cost-reward ratio of a benchmark can be very positive indeed (for detailed remarks on benchmarking, see below).

[26]In the interest of brevity, we rigorously stuck to an extremely short presentation of the main facts. In practice, you will generally have to elaborate a little more on the individual functions to avoid ambiguity with respect to the classification of the entities.

[27]For very small companies, it will even be feasible to limit the functional and risk analysis to a respective illustration ("star-chart").

entertainment for everyone" which is built on combining innovative technologies and competitive pricing. It was further established that the main drivers of the business profit) are the product development function and efficient manufacturing process, as well as a coherent communications and marketing strategy. In the following, the functions essential for Prima's value creation are examined chronologically, i.e., from research to after-sales.

Functions

Research and Production

Technological developments (digitization, etc.) have a significant impact on the products of the Prima Group (comparatively short life cycle). To attain the position of a technology leader within the industry, Prima devotes a substantial share of its annual budget to research and development. Prima has developed production processes in the past, which form the sustainable basis for comparatively advantageous cost structures. All development and production processes are carried out by Prima. The value-added attribute to these functions for the success of the Prima Group is high.

Procurement

Prima's procurement department is responsible for all major strategic and operational procurement functions. Prima is responsible for the functions aimed at realizing the advantages of the optimization of volume discounts and delivery conditions. The local subsidiaries assume procurement functions only on a selective basis for some product groups on the local market (subject to approval by Prima). Overall, the procurement function is of medium importance for total value added.

Quality Assurance

Analogous to the division of functions outlined for Procurement, Prima assumes all essential strategic functions regarding quality control. For operational execution, however, functions are increasingly provided by the foreign subsidiaries (in particular support for certification procedures and installations), with the share of orders placed with local testing institutes for technically comparatively simple tests being successively replaced by their own testing procedures. Prima samples and monitors compliance with the testing procedures.

Logistics and Warehousing[28]

Daily supply capability and the storage of an extensive product range are essential competitive factors for the Prima Group, which can only be ensured by a modern logistics system. A modern logistics system also forms an indispensable basis for minimizing storage costs.

Sales and Marketing

The sales and marketing functions contribute to substantial added value for companies focused on retail customers. Prima's sales department is responsible for all essential strategic sales functions, i.e., branding and strategic decisions on sales channels. While Prima also determines the general pricing policy, the foreign subsidiaries are given a comparatively high degree of leeway in their negotiations so that they can make the best possible use of their special knowledge and connections on the local market.

After-Sales

Prima defines all essential parameters and service-level agreements. The subsidiaries act as local partners within the given parameters (first- and second-level support). The importance of after-sales as an ancillary process for the total value added is evaluated as being medium.

Management and Administration

The management of the foreign subsidiaries is largely handled by local staff (local accounting, customs clearance, communication with authorities and external consultants, etc.). Prima supports its subsidiaries in the areas of general administration (management) and IT. Overall, only a small contribution to value added can be attributed to these administrative services.[29]

---

[28]The description of the Warehousing and Logistics function provided by this case study can be considered insufficient, especially because, first, the total value-added attributable to this function is not explicitly put into perspective and, and second, the functions are not delineated between Prima and the Subsidiaries. We will later see that such ambiguity can result in additional risk. One advantage of compiling a star-chart is that it forces you to revisit the consistency of the functional analysis. In the case at hand, additional explanations were required to evaluate the logistics and warehousing function. A possible explanation here could have been: Prima operates a state-of-the art logistics center and is responsible for ensuring efficient freight and transport processes, while the local subsidiaries generally outsource local logistics (delivery).

[29]This statement is relevant in view of the required level of aggregation. Considering that the services provided by Prima are merely of supporting nature, it will generally be feasible to argue that a segmented analysis is not required—this will, however, also depend on the respective transaction volumes. The explanations provided above, however, suggest that the local entities have substantial local capacity—so that the transaction volume for centralized services is likely limited.

Risks

As highlighted above, an evaluation of the relevant business risks is important for ensuring the tax viability of the functional and risk analysis.[30]

Research and Development Risk

Research and Development Risk describes the risk that the research activities may not generate any result, i.e., marketable product. Due to the high level of respective investments (see above) and the substantial degree of uncertainty as to whether these investments will translate into successfully marketable products, research and development risks are substantial for the Prima Group. All respective risks are borne by Prima. The success of the Prima products on the market strongly depends on the quality of development activities performed by Prima.

Product Liability and Quality Risk

Product liability risk is incurred when the manufactured or distributed products fail to perform at accepted or advertised standards. As both Prima and the local subsidiaries provide after-sales services, both are responsible for the functionality of their products. While these risks are generally shared and borne by both parties, Prima, acting as the sole manufacturing unit of the group, will recompensate the local subsidiaries for any malfunctions attributable to manufacturing.[31] Should one party act negligently, the costs will internally be allocated respectively.

[30] A separate analysis of risks (and assets) can be deliberately forgone when dealing with fairly "straightforward" transactions. The basic assumption in this context is that the risks and assets will ideally "follow" the functions and that therefore a separate evaluation would be redundant—i.e., it would add an additional layer of complexity without substantially enhancing the reliability of the analysis and the resulting classification. For more detailed explanations and practical implementation, see the value chain analysis tool available for download. Even though these assumptions would apply in the case of the Prima Group, we found it preferable to provide you with an explicit description of the relevant risks—i.e., provide you with a complete picture.

[31] Admittedly, the explanation is somewhat vague. It is, however, not uncommon to encounter such situations in practice, especially in SMEs. In the case of Prima, however, there does not seem to exist a glaring misalignment between functions and risks, i.e. Prima performs all production functions as well as the strategic functions regarding quality assurance—hence, it seems to be plausible that Prima will bear the respective risks by recompensing the local subsidiaries for costs related to faulty manufacturing. While it would be highly recommendable to clarify the allocation of product liability risks (i.e. by amending existing contracts or drafting new contracts), the potential for (aggressive) transfer pricing adjustments seems limited.

Market Risk

Market risk occurs when a firm is subject to adverse sales conditions due to either increased competition in the marketplace, adverse demand conditions within the market, or the inability to develop markets or position products to service-targeted customers. Market risk includes, but is not limited to, obsolescence risk and price-level decline risk. Prima incurs all cost for the global brand building and related services. Since the additional investments for local marketing by Prima are limited to supporting local entities during the market-entry phase, the risks related to the local market are primarily borne by the local subsidiaries. The price-setting, however, includes country-specific discount rates, which, while not completely shielding the local subsidiaries from market risk, factually leads to Prima bearing the bulk of the respective risks.[32]

Customer Credit Risk

Customer credit risk is borne when products are supplied, or services performed for customers and payment for the same is deferred to a later date. Credit risks are comparatively limited for the business of the Prima Group (i.e., with a default rate below 2%). The credit risk is borne by the local subsidiaries who hold the contract with the local customers (except for the commission business, for which the compensation to be paid to the local subsidiaries is calculated based on invoices issued by Prima rather than based on payments received. Hence, Prima factually bears the credit risk).

Functional and Risk Profile

Based on the preceding analysis, it is feasible to establish a functional and risk profile, which illustrates how functions and risks are distributed between the group companies. In addition, the functional and risk profile illustrates which of the functions are to be considered as key value drivers and the intensity with which the respective entity contributes to the specific functions.

The functional and risk profile illustrated in Fig. 2.4 is a so-called "star chart," which is commonly used by transfer pricing professionals and can be found in almost any transfer pricing documentation. The analysis is focused on delineating the value added of each function (risk) by each company in relation to the transaction

[32]Whether or not this statement is accurate, i.e., whether the resulting transfer prices are commensurate with the arm's length principle, can only be assessed in the context of the comparability analysis. Considering that the analysis here leaves a rather high degree of ambiguity regarding such a vital (sensitive) issue, we would strongly recommend providing additional explanations when encountering a similar situation in practice. Compared to the product liability and quality risk (see previous footnote), the ambiguity regarding the market risk seems much more severe in the case of Prima.

Prima Group – Functional and Risk Profile		
Function	**Prima**	**Subsidiaries**
Research/Production	+++++	
Procurement	++	+
Quality Assurance	++	+
Logistics/Warehousing	++	+
Sales/Marketing	+ + + +	++
After Sales	++	+
Management / Administration	+	+
Risks	**Prima**	**Subsidiaries**
Research and Development	+++++	
Product Liability and Quality	++	+
Market Risk	+++	++
Customer Credit Risk	+	+

Fig. 2.4 Functional and risk profile of the Prima Group. (source: own illustration)

"sale of products." Based on the relevant facts and circumstances, i.e., the subordinated or complementary nature of the services (loans) provided, a separate functional and risk analysis is not required (at this point). Each function and risk is allocated up to five points (+).[33] The amount of points reflects the intensity with which each company performs the respective functions (or assumes the corresponding risk). The sum of points allocated to a specific function across all group companies reflects the importance of this function for the entire value chain.

Based on the functional and risk profile, Prima, which is responsible for all relevant strategic decisions and performs the functions that are decisive for the success of the company, can be classified as the "entrepreneur" of the Prima

[33]There are almost infinitesimal options to assign weights to the different functions—with some being better than others, but ultimately, it is a matter of taste as well. Under no circumstance, however, should you refrain from assigning (plausible) weights, as this will render the analysis factually worthless and cause severe harm. For a detailed example, please refer to the complementary Excel-Tool, which includes a detailed "how-not-to" example based on an OECD case study. A further "how not to example" in the context of Prima is provided at the end of this section.

OECD Guidelines 2017, Paragraph 3.18
When applying a cost plus, resale price or transactional net margin method [...], it is necessary to choose the party to the transaction for which a financial indicator (mark-up on costs, gross margin, or net profit indicator) is tested. The **choice of the tested party should be consistent with the functional analysis** of the transaction. As a general rule, the tested party is the one to which a transfer pricing method can be applied in the most reliable manner and for which the most reliable comparables can be found, i.e. **it will most often be the one that has the less complex functional analysis.**

Fig. 2.5 Defining the tested party (source: OECD)

Group. The functions performed by the subsidiaries are focused on local sales and marketing and are of comparatively minor importance for total value added. In addition, the subsidiaries are partially shielded from market risks. Consequently, the subsidiaries can be classified as "routine companies" (e.g., limited risk distributors). Again, please refer to the **complementary Excel Tools**[34] for pragmatic guidance on how to quantify value-added contributions to verify that your quantitative assessment of individual functions results in an accurate (plausible) image of the business model.

One should not be too caught-up by labels at this point. Specifically, one should be careful when using labels such as "limited risk distributor" or "fully fledged distributor," as sometimes tax authorities tend to interpret respective labels rather restrictively; i.e., you might face additional discussions if "your" limited risk distributor does not match the textbook definition applied by the authorities.[35] Their generic nature renders the categories "entrepreneur" and "routine" to be highly advantageous, as they allow for an illustration of the guiding principle embodied in Paragraph 1.51 of the OECD Guidelines.[36] As it contributes the bulk of the total value added, an entrepreneur will be entitled to the bulk of profits (losses), i.e., the "residual profit," which remains after the routine entities have received an arm's length remuneration (compensation) for their services. Hence, the profits allocated to an entrepreneur will generally be much more volatile compared to those of a routine entity. The OECD captures this logic in the concept of the "tested party," which is defined in Fig. 2.5:

Looking at the functional and risk profile for the Prima Group, it should be evident, at one glance, that the subsidiaries exhibit the less complex functional

---

[34]**The Excel Tool ("Value Chain Analysis") is available in http://extras.springer.com for download on the homepage of Transfer Pricing in Lesson.**

[35]Please also note that these labels are at least somewhat fuzzy and that there is no international consensus on the definition (at least not in the realm of transfer pricing); the OECD refers to specific labels such as a limited risk distributor merely in the context of Chapter IX. These references, however, are made without providing a clear-cut definition but rather provide a case-study-type of delineation between a limited risk distributor and a full-fledged distributor.

[36]Note: Various countries such as Germany have explicitly integrated the categories "entrepreneur" and "routine entity" into their transfer pricing regulations. Germany, being Germany, has created a third, in-between, category, the so-called hybrid entity. Such an ostensibly more "fine-grained" categorization is, however, rather disadvantageous in practice. In this context, the most notable disadvantage is that the TNMM may not be utilized for "hybrid" entities.

profile and would thus be chosen as the tested party. The basic rationale here is rather simple; the entrepreneur (Prima) performs highly complex and value-added functions and will, due to these unique and valuable contributions, be difficult to compare to independent third parties, whereas it will often be feasible to identify distribution companies that are (somewhat) comparable to the subsidiaries of Prima. More complex considerations can and should be deferred to the comparability analysis.

The functional and risk profile created for the Prima Group will be generally sufficient because it does provide us with a viable basis for choosing a tested party. It may not be perfect. And, yes, I can almost hear your critical comments. And you are right. The above analysis leaves much to be desired and various key aspects remain ambiguous.[37] But, how severe is the shortcoming really? Well, I would argue it is not such a big deal after all. Why? Because the classification of the entities seems to be rather hard to refute for any tax auditor. While it is conceivable that one would have to quibble about some of the ambiguities,[38] it is simply inconceivable that a tax auditor would try to challenge the classification as such. Feasible "quick-fixes" to the above analysis would be (non-exclusive list):

- Defining research and production as two distinct categories => as both would be allocated a substantial weight which would be exclusively assigned to Prima, the contrast between Prima and the subsidiaries would be further enhanced. An important take-away here is that you should avoid listing too many supplementary or sub-functions; i.e., the quantity of functions would threaten to dilute the value allocated to the key functions
- For sales and marketing applying two distinct categories (or sub-categories) would be also feasible. In this context, however, it would be required to provide a more cautious delineation between strategic and operative functions, i.e., the quality or economic significance of the (unique and valuable) inputs of Prima would outweigh the more quantitatively relevant operative functions of the subsidiaries.[39]
- Further analyzing the market risks borne by the subsidiaries. As mentioned in an earlier footnote, the remaining ambiguity relating to the market risk is the Achilles heel of the analysis. While addressing this issue is not necessarily a "quick fix," it is the one issue you should focus on here—quibbling about other issues (i.e., should a second "+" be assigned to after sales functions performed by the subsidiaries will only sidetrack you here).

[37] I have highlighted several ambiguities myself and will further elaborate on the impact as well as on additional ambiguities below.

[38] In the case at hand, the degree of quibbling would depend on the financial results, i.e., whether it is worthwhile to quibble, and it is safe to assume that the quibbling would be confined to the comparability analysis (which, as we shall see below, implied much smaller risks than challenges to the functional and risk analysis).

[39] Note: We have thus far not put specific emphasis on the role of intangibles. If only one party contributes to unique and valuable intangibles, integrating these in the analysis will often result in a much clearer functional profile—as the functional profile above is, however, deemed to be sufficiently clear, the discussions of intangibles are deferred to the more advanced sections.

Prima Group – Functional and Risk Profile – "how NOT to" example		
Function	**Prima**	**Subsidiaries**
Research/Production	+	
Procurement	+	+
Quality Assurance	+	+
Logistics	+	+
Warehousing	+	+
Sales	+	+
Marketing	+	+
Negotiation		+
After Sales	+	+
Management	+	+
Administration	+	+

Fig. 2.6 How NOT to illustrate a functional and risk profile (source: own illustration)

Again, the **value chain analysis tool**[40] will provide you with further details, including step-by-step guidance.

The following "**how NOT to**" or "worst case" example depicted in Fig. 2.6 is intended to provide you with an additional perspective on the advantages of ensuring an unambiguous functional profile.

The "how NOT to" functional profile is arguably in line with the outlined facts and circumstances. The chosen presentation of the functional profile, i.e., neglecting to assign weights to functions and fragmenting closely related (sub-)functions, will, however, almost always result in a blurred profile. In practice, such an ambiguous profile is bound to (literally) cause more damage than good. It is no longer feasible to identify the tested party at a glance. Hence, a tax auditor will be forced to dig deeper into the functional analysis. In interpreting the analysis, he is bound to look for weaknesses in the analysis that allow him to challenge the identification of the tested party (and by extension) the selection of the appropriate transfer pricing method.[41] In

[40]**The Excel Tool is available in http://extras.springer.com for download on the homepage of Transfer Pricing in Lesson**.

[41]Note: This is not intended as a derogative comment to tax auditors. They naturally have an agenda and are in no way obliged or incentivized to make interpretation in favor of the taxpayer. This is just how the game is played and most people can appreciate this without bitterness. Submitting a poor functional and risks profile is akin to scoring in your own goal, i.e., while the opposition may not

the case at hand, a tax auditor could challenge the "routine" classification of the Prima subsidiary, arguing that the subsidiary contributes just as much value (based on the number of assigned points "+") as Prima and should, consequently, be entitled to an appropriate share of the residual profits. Depending on the proportion of the residual profits, this could lead to painful transfer pricing (profit) adjustments—emphasizing, again, that a good functional and risk analysis will reduce transfer pricing related risks by about 75%. We will look at numerical examples during the following case study sections.

An unambiguous functional profile also has the advantage of providing a basis for the decision on an appropriate level of aggregation of the controlled transactions. In the case at hand, the functional and risk analysis clarified that the services rendered by Prima to the subsidiaries are of supplementary and subordinated nature.[42] Having identified the Prima subsidiaries as routine companies, they will (likely) be chosen as the tested parties for whom a financial indicator (most likely a net margin) will be compared to that of independent parties (see OECD Guidelines, Paragraph 3.18). While we will talk about financial indicators ("profit-level indicators") during subsequent sections, it should be noted (from a practitioner's perspective) that the respective comparison will often be based on P&L level data—as segmented financial data are not available for independent parties. Hence, when conducting a comparability analysis for the Prima subsidiaries, the arm's length nature of the service fee (mark-up on full costs) will be included in the evaluation of the total net margin resulting from the sales activities.[43] The aggregation could be easily justified by emphasizing that in the case of Prima, the ostensible separate transactions are closely linked and of continuous nature and that, therefore, they cannot be evaluated on a separate basis (with reference to the OECD Guidelines, Paragraph 3.9[44]).

---

exactly pat themselves on the back, they will certainly be happy to take advantage of the opportunity.

[42]That statement is feasible here even without knowing the transaction volumes. In case the transaction volumes for the service transaction would later turn out to be disproportionately high, this should trigger additional scrutiny in the sense that the accuracy of the functional analysis should be double-checked.

[43]Note: As the "net margin" is to be understood as the EBIT margins, the rationalization of integrating the transactions will not easily extend to including financial transactions. While the evaluation of financial transactions will also have to consider the broad economic conditions of the taxpayers, they will generally be evaluated as a separate analysis—in any case, however, you should be careful to ensure that interest payments do not cannibalize the routine profits of your tested party—for details on financial transactions, please refer to the "advanced" section.

[44]Note: In the case of Prima, at least for the simple setup discussed thus far, it would also be feasible to argue (again based on Paragraph 3.9) that it is impractical to determine pricing for each individual product or transaction, i.e., the arm's length nature of the compensation of the "services" rendered by Prima could appropriately be included in the net margin agreed for the sales transaction.

Box 2.1 Restating the Lesson

The Functional and Risk Analysis Is the Heart of the Arm's Length Principle

The functional and risk analysis forces you to dissect the business model of the MNE and is vital to never losing sight of the reality of a specific business. The resulting identification of the tested party constitutes an intuitive mechanism for making a fundamental decision with respect to an arm's length allocation of profits, i.e., an allocation that is proportionate to the value contributions of the parties.

Even at this coarse-grained level of analysis, it should be evident that the arm's length principle is not a means for tax avoidance but rather a pragmatic and comparatively transparent mechanism for appropriately "translating" a specific business model into a tax viable transfer pricing structure.

Form an economic (business) perspective, a transacting party that can easily be substituted (i.e., because it really does not bring something unique to the table) will not be in a position to claim a substantial share of the total profit resulting from the respective business activity. It will simply be in an inferior bargaining position. Like any independent contractor with sufficient capacity, such party will readily accept a remuneration that covers its costs plus a small profit in exchange for rendering services on behalf of a principal. Now, if we can agree that such an arrangement is sensible and reflects a common behavior between independent parties, we should also agree that there is nothing onerous about adopting this logic for tax purposes. Why should a comparatively "simple" (routine) entity share in the residual profits of an MNE? Establishing a local service provider and remunerating this entity with small but stable profits seems hardly something that could be labeled "aggressive tax planning."

In cases where it is feasible to identify a clear-cut tested party, we should therefore be confident that the application of a one-sided transfer pricing method, i.e., a method focused on ensuring an arm's length remuneration for the tested party, will result in a profit allocation that is "appropriate" from an economic as well as from a tax perspective. The functional analysis in turn is a compulsory component of each transfer pricing documentation and can be verified comparatively easily by the tax authorities.

Again, there is nothing "artificial" about the arm's length principle and a functional and risk analysis. The foundation of the analysis and the subsequent selection of a tested party is ALWAYS the specific business model of a MNE. The first and foremost task of a transfer pricing consultant is therefore to understand the business model of his client and ensure that the model is accurately translated into a tax viable transfer pricing structure.

Chapter 3
Applying the Lesson to Basic Transactions

By working through Chap. 2, we have laid the foundation for ensuring a viable transfer pricing system. To be 100% clear, understanding the relevant economic circumstances and conducting a functional and risk analysis, including the choice of a tested party, account for eliminating about 75% of transfer pricing-related risks. The accurate documentation and analysis of the economic fundamentals will resonate throughout the comparability analysis. Most importantly, the functional analysis provides a clear indication of the general profit allocation, i.e., which party will be entitled to entrepreneurial (residual) profits/losses. Obviously, a more detailed analysis, i.e., a comparability analysis, will now be required to evaluate whether the transfer prices are commensurate with the arm's length principle.[1]

The OECD provides a nine-step best practice approach for conducting a comparability analysis, as summarized in Fig. 3.1.

Thus far we have covered Step 2 and the first part of Step 3.[2] We will now commence by focusing on the second part of Step 3, i.e., selecting an appropriate transfer pricing method to the circumstances of a specific case. In order to make any decision on the most appropriate method, we must first look in the toolbox and understand which transfer pricing methods are at our disposal. In discussing the method selection, we will also address the vital issue of "comparability."[3]

[1]Note: As pointed out by the IRS in the context of the IRS Treas. Reg. § 1.482-1: "Allocation of income and deductions among taxpayers: "A functional analysis is not a pricing method and does not itself determine the arm's length result for the controlled transaction under review".

[2]At first glance, the nine-step approach may look to be complex and complicated. But, again, Step 2 (broad-based understanding of the economic circumstances) and Step 3 (functional analysis) are the core elements. Step 4 through Step 9 are, as we shall see, mere "technicalities." Performing these steps will require proper utilization of available analytical tools, but ultimately the analysis amounts to quantifying the profit allocation which is systematically predetermined by the functional analysis. The determination of the years to be covered is only seldom a question of practical relevance, at least insofar as it relates to systemic risks.

[3]By discussing the significant comparability factors (Step 3 of the OECD best practices), we will already, at least implicitly, address the most important aspects of Step 4 through Step 8.

O. Treidler, *Transfer Pricing in One Lesson*, Management for Professionals,
https://doi.org/10.1007/978-3-030-25085-0_3

OECD Guidelines 2017, Paragraph 3.4

Step 1: Determination of years to be covered.

Step 2: Broad-based analysis of the taxpayer's circumstances.

Step 3: Understanding the controlled transaction(s) under examination, based in particular on a functional analysis, in order to choose the tested party (where needed), the most appropriate transfer pricing method to the circumstances of the case, [...] and to identify the significant comparability factors that should be taken into account.

Step 4: Review of existing internal comparables, if any.

Step 5: Determination of available sources of information on external comparables where such external comparables are needed taking into account their relative reliability.

Step 6: Selection of the most appropriate transfer pricing method and, depending on the method, determination of the relevant financial indicator (e.g. determination of the relevant net profit indicator in case of a transactional net margin method).

Step 7: Identification of potential comparables: determining the key characteristics to be met by any uncontrolled transaction in order to be regarded as potentially comparable, based on the relevant factors identified in Step 3 and in accordance with the comparability factors set forth at Section D.1 of Chapter I.

Step 8: Determination of and making comparability adjustments where appropriate.

Step 9: Interpretation and use of data collected, determination of the arm's length remuneration.

Fig. 3.1 Step-by-step best practices for conducting a comparability analysis (source: OECD)

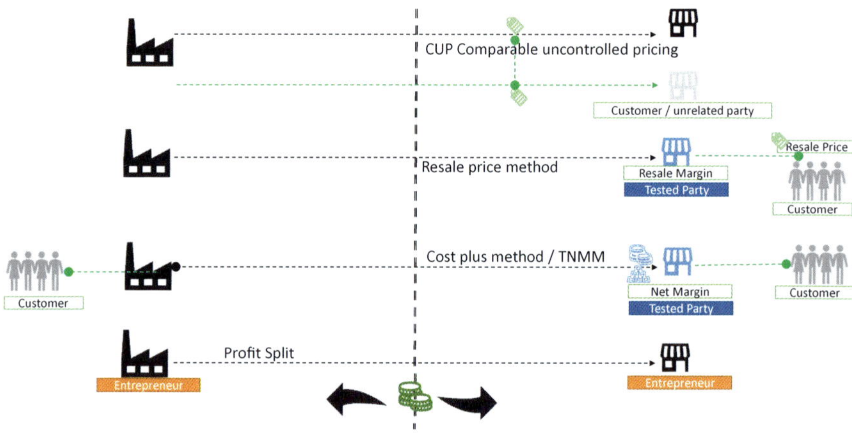

Fig. 3.2 Transfer pricing methods: overview (Source: own illustration)

Before looking at individual methods in detail, it is worthwhile to, at least briefly, glance at the "big picture." Considering that we have only five methods in our "transfer pricing tool box," the big picture is not really all that complicated. Figure 3.2 provides an overview of the transfer pricing methods to which you can always return when you want to compare the main characteristics of the different methods, i.e., object of comparison and the classification of the transacting parties.

Transfer pricing methods are "flexible" and will allow you to find a best fit for your business model; you should, however, never use them "arbitrarily." While the feasibility of the CUP will heavily depend on ensuring a sufficient degree of comparability of the price for specific products or services (see Sect. 3.1), the feasibility of all other methods will depend primarily on the functional profile of the transacting parties; i.e., while comparability is a highly complex issue in the context of the CUP (i.e., accounting for many comparability factors such as transaction volumes, terms of trade, timing, etc.), the assessment of comparability when

OECD Guidelines 2017, Paragraph 2.2

The selection of a transfer pricing method always aims at finding the **most appropriate method for a particular case.** For this purpose, the selection process should take account of the respective strengths and weaknesses of the OECD recognized methods; the appropriateness of the method considered in view of the nature of the controlled transaction, **determined in particular through a functional analysis**; the availability of reliable information (in particular on uncontrolled comparables) needed to apply the selected method [...]; and the degree of comparability between controlled and uncontrolled transactions, including the reliability of comparability adjustments that may be needed to eliminate material differences between them.

Fig. 3.3 Selection of the most appropriate method—no hierarchy of methods (source: OECD)

applying the other methods will, at least predominantly, revolve around comparability of functions.

One question that is frequently debated is whether there is a hierarchical order to the methods. The answer is, at least to a certain extent, a moving target and tricky to generalize. Conceptually, the CUP can be considered the "most direct" method for evaluating the arm's length nature of a specific price. Hence, at least historically, tax authorities often had a "preference" for a CUP.[4] Recently, however, there is a clear tendency toward a consensus on the OECD Guidelines presented in Paragraph 2.2 (see Fig. 3.3).

The OECD concludes Paragraph 2.2 with a healthy dose of pragmatism, namely, that "No one method is suitable in every possible situation, nor is it necessary to prove that a particular method is not suitable under the circumstances" (see also Paragraph 2.8). When dealing with more complex situations, especially a situation in which the result of the functional and risk analysis shows the functional profile of your tested party to substantially exceed a strict routine categorization, it will, however, generally pay dividends to go through the motions of proving that a particular method is not applicable. While there is no point in mechanically walking through each method,[5] there are cases in which proactively excluding a method is an excellent way to mitigate your transfer pricing risk.[6]

[4]In some transfer pricing regulations, such preference is explicitly stated; i.e., the IRS Treas. Reg. § 1.482-1(c)(2)(i) states that: "Thus, an analysis under the comparable uncontrolled price method will generally be more reliable than analyses obtained under other methods if the analysis is based on closely comparable uncontrolled transactions, because such an analysis can be expected to achieve a higher degree of comparability and be susceptible to fewer differences than analyses under other methods."

[5]Note: You still find quite a number of transfer pricing documentations describing each method in detail (which is a waste of paper really, as a reference to the OECD Guidelines would be just as fine) and which then go on to offer some rather half-hearted explanation on why each, save the selected, method is not applicable; i.e., it sometimes makes for awkward reading when selecting the TNMM and simultaneously presenting an argument on why the cost-plus method is not applicable (as will be shown, these methods are conceptually rather similar—which also, to a more limited degree, applies to the Resale Price Method). Yes, as far as I know the US-Regs § 1.482-1(c) stipulate that each method must be reviewed (excluded)—but really, such regulations should be consigned to the dustbin of history.

[6]The most important cases, as will be shown below, are those in which the applicability of the profit split method is potentially up for discussions with the tax authorities.

To wrap up the "big picture," I want to provide you with a list of some additional "nice-to-know" aspects regarding the selection of an appropriate transfer pricing method:

- Pursuant to the OECD Guidelines (Paragraph 2.9), MNEs are free to apply Methods that are not defined by the OECD. For a limited number of cases, taking advantage of this provision might be beneficial. You should, however, tread cautiously in these cases, as tax authorities are likely to be in "high alert" mode when they encounter something "unorthodox."[7]
- As indicated above (implied in the guidance of Paragraph 2.2), MNEs are not required to apply more than one method. It is, however, in their discretion to apply two methods for establishing arm's length prices in complex situations (Paragraph 2.12). When you can demonstrate that two methods support the same price (i.e., overlapping arm's length ranges), this will obviously greatly improve your chances of successfully defending your transfer prices.
- While a pragmatic application of the arm's length principle is feasible when observing the basic parameters outlined in this chapter (always referring to the principle of proportionality), there are "limits" to the acceptable degree of simplification. A clear case in being "out of bounds" is when MNEs set their transfer prices with reference to unadjusted average returns within their industry (see Paragraph 1.40 of the OECD-GL).
- Having a contract in place to document the business relationship between two related parties is always positive. You should, however, never base your argument for selecting a transfer pricing method on (merely) referring to contractual provisions (see Paragraphs 1.42–1.50). You will always have to clarify the actual conduct of the parties (i.e., present a functional and risk analysis).

3.1 The Comparable Uncontrolled Price (CUP) Method

When reading Paragraph 2.2 of the OECD Guidelines and listing to the discussion of a hierarchal order of transfer pricing methods—with the CUP Method (see Fig. 3.4) being placed at the top of the pyramid—one might get the impression that the CUP is the most straightforward and reliable method, i.e., sort of a default method. Alas, in practice, nothing could be further from the truth. Simply put, a CUP is THE most

[7]When applying a so-called other method, there are decent odds that your tax auditor has never encountered such a situation before; i.e., you should provide extremely detailed explanations. I would also suggest that most other methods will ultimately be "variants" of the profit split method (which will almost always be applicable for a secondary analysis—see the respective remarks in Sect. 3.4). Please also note that the use of "rules of thumb" is strongly discouraged, because, as correctly pointed out by the OECD (Paragraph 2.10), rules of thumb do not provide an adequate substitute for a functional and comparability analysis—I will, however, make some comments in the "advanced lessons" on the conditions under which certain rules of thumb (i.e., the so-called Goldscheider-Rule or the so-called Knoppe-Formula) can be beneficial.

OECD Guidelines 2017, Paragraph 2.14
The CUP method compares the price charged for property or services transferred in a controlled transaction to the price charged for property or services transferred in a comparable uncontrolled transaction in **comparable circumstances.**

Fig. 3.4 The CUP method (source: OECD)

difficult method to handle, as the appropriate scope for the application of a CUP is the most narrowly (restrictively) defined of all methods.[8] Pursuant to the OECD Guidelines (Paragraph 2.15), an uncontrolled transaction is comparable to a controlled transaction for purposes of the CUP method, if one of the following conditions is met:

(a) *None of the* ***differences*** *(if any) between the transactions being compared or between the enterprises undertaking those transactions could* ***materially affect*** *the price in the open market.*
(b) *Reasonably* ***accurate adjustments*** *can be made to* ***eliminate the material effects*** *of such differences*

While the OECD also states that "*Where it is possible to locate comparable uncontrolled transactions, the CUP method is the most direct and reliable way to apply the arm's length principle. Consequently, in such cases the CUP method is preferable over all other methods*" (also Paragraph 2.15), it is the restrictive interpretation of the "key terms" included in the two conditions which render it incredibly hard to find a sufficiently comparable uncontrolled transaction. With respect to the conditions listed above, the OECD provides the following interpretation:

(a) "Differences" are to be interpreted in a broader context; i.e., not only product comparability is to be considered but rather all business activities that are relevant for the transaction. Even "minor differences" could materially affect the price, even though "[. . .] *the business activities undertaken may be sufficiently similar to generate the same overall profit margin*" (Paragraph 2.16). The, arguably, most "revealing" provision contained in the OECD Guidelines with respect to the limited scope for applying the CUP is to be found in Paragraph 2.18, namely, that "[. . .] *the CUP method would generally be an appropriate transfer pricing method for establishing the arm's length price for the transfer of commodities [. . .]. The reference to 'commodities' shall be understood to encompass physical products for which a quoted price is used as a reference by independent parties in the industry to set prices in uncontrolled transactions.*"[9] The OECD further emphasizes that even if an appropriate quoted

[8]Note: There may well be various national regulations allowing a wider (less restrictive) scope for applying the CUP, but the assumption here is that in the medium to long term, most regulations will be closer aligned with the post-BEPS OECD Guidelines.

[9]Note: Even the appropriateness of a "quoted price" is subject to a highly restrictive interpretation; i.e. acceptability for tax purposes will depend on the extent to which the quoted price is widely and routinely used in the ordinary course of business in the industry to negotiate prices (Paragraph 2.19)—in other words, it does not help you much to be creative in identifying external comparable

price is identified for a specific commodity, the MNE will have to ensure comparability of the economically relevant characteristics (i.e., the physical features and quality of the commodity; the volumes traded as well as the timing and terms of delivery, transportation, insurance, and foreign currency terms)—see OECD Guidelines Paragraph 2.20.

(b) Considering that relevant "differences" are interpreted in an extremely broad context, it is evident that there will be an almost inevitable need to perform adjustments. In the examples provided by the OECD, it is emphasized that even provided that two transactions are identical in terms of timing, stage within production/distribution chain, and other relevant economic conditions, adjustments will be required for differences in product quality (i.e., Columbian vs. Brazilian Coffee). For commodity transactions, that emphasis seems sensible as minor differences in quality will have an immediate effect on the (transfer) price; i.e., on the 29th of June, "Columbian Milds" were quoted at 136.24 (US cents/lb) by the International Coffee Organization, while "Brazilian Naturals" were quoted at 112.17 (US cents/lb).[10] For noncommodity transactions, however, it will not be feasible to obtain public data that is commensurate with the OECD's restrictive interpretation of a quoted price. Hence, performing sufficiently "accurate adjustments" to **eliminate** the **material effects of differences** in noncommodity transactions constitutes a tall order indeed. Often, it will only be feasible to conduct an "internal CUP"; i.e., to compare the prices of identical products sold by an MNE to related as well as to unrelated parties. Even in cases where data for an internal CUP is available, however, there will obviously have to be adjustments for differences in terms of trade (incoterms) or differences in volume (discounts).[11] While these adjustments will generally be feasible, the "degree of accuracy" will remain subject of debate (i.e., be "risk" in an audit).

Figure 3.5 illustrates the textbook (OECD) version of a CUP (based on the OECD examples referenced above).

It is one of the most curious but consistent experiences made by transfer pricing consultants that their clients tend to underestimate the degree of comparability required for applying a CUP. One reason for this might be that the professional background of managers in charge of setting transfer pricing is often in business controlling or management accounting. For the purposes of management

data in this context—hence, why bother. Also, it is worthwhile to note that the limited scope of applying the CUP to "commodity transactions" is also repeated in Paragraph 2.21.

[10]The quotations were downloaded from the ICO homepage on the 24th of July 2018. The example of quotes for coffee prices provides strong support for the OECD's insistence on "timing issues" when performing a CUP for commodities (Paragraph 2.22), i.e. Brazilian Naturals were quoted at 121.95 (US cents/lb) on June 1st.

[11]Also, differences in the business relationship need to be considered. As seen in Chap. 2, a myopic transaction-by-transaction analysis will not constitute a solid basis for assessing the arm's length nature of the agreed transfer prices.

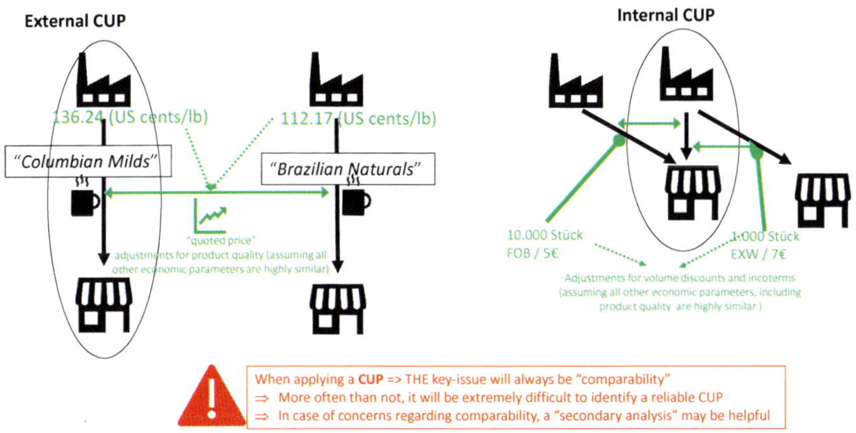

Fig. 3.5 Textbook examples for a CUP (source: own illustration—based on OECD)

accounting, it often seems advantageous to set the transfer prices by looking at prices agreed between the MNE and unrelated companies (so-called "internal comparables").[12] From the management accounting perspective, the importance of a functional and risk profile for tax purposes as well as a corresponding classification of the entities is likely to be perceived as being too "abstract" or "artificial." While it is perfectly understandable that the tax-specific categories tend to be discounted as being too artificial, it is important to question whether the management accounting perspective is not prone to adopt an idealized view of the comparability of market prices. The following questions could be asked to determine whether market prices can be adopted for management accounting purposes[13]:

- Do the transacting business units have (uninhibited) access to the open market?
- Are the external and internal products or services equivalent?
- Are all synergy effects (positive and negative) included in the transfer prices?
- Are transfer prices adjusted to reflect short-term price fluctuation on the market?

[12]Note: This is often the case when the MNE utilizes a so-called "Master Price List" that is applied for internal and external distributors. In some, less frequent, cases the prices are also determined based on data observed on the market (so-called external comparables). The use of such external comparables (if available at all) is, however, also discouraged by the management accounting literature—as there is no way in determining whether the competitor is operating efficiently and whether using the prices as a reference will provide sensible incentives for an efficient resource allocation. Also, remember from the previous section, using unadjusted industry averages to determine tax viable transfer prices is explicitly discouraged by the OECD.

[13]The questions geared toward uncovering that management accounting is prone to adopt an idealized notion of market prices are derived from Hanken et al. (2017). Unfortunately (to my knowledge), this book is only available in German. The book is a great source of reference for any advanced practitioner dealing with questions at the critical junction between a management accounting and tax perspective on transfer pricing.

When being confronted with these questions, most management accountants are likely to concede that there are indeed differences between market prices and transfer prices that would require (additional) adjustments—especially when the degree of comparability and accuracy of adjustments required for tax purposes is explained by referring to the OECD examples illustrated above.

The key takeaway, and main theme, of this book is that when adopting an entrepreneurial approach to transfer pricing, the chasm between tax perspective and the management accounting perspective can be overcome—or at least there is some sensible middle ground here. Obviously, getting hung up on the restrictive tax perspective reflected in the OECD perspective on the CUP method would practically disqualify the use of market prices as reference for transfer pricing purposes. On the other hand, an all-too-careless insistence on giving preference to the management perspective, especially when remaining stuck in an idealized view on market prices, will put the tax viability of your transfer pricing system in jeopardy. To explore the middle ground, it is worthwhile to embrace the guidance provided by the OECD in Paragraph 2.17: "Practical considerations dictate a more flexible approach to enable the CUP method to be used and to be supplemented as necessary by other appropriate methods, [. . .]. Every effort should be made to adjust the data so that it may be used appropriately in a CUP method".

Hence, when evaluating the possible application of the CUP with your colleagues/clients, the following points may provide a sensible basis for your discussion **(the "CUP decision tree")**:

1. Are we looking at a commodity transaction?
   (a) If "yes", great => to dos: (1) identify a "quoted price," (2) double-check comparability (be strict and remember "timing issues" are especially sensitive for commodities), and (3) conduct adjustment payments (if required).
   (b) If "no," don't worry => to dos: (1) acknowledge that conducting a reliable (tax viable) external CUP for a non-commodity transaction will be difficult, and (2) keep following the decision tree.
2. Can we identify an internal CUP?
   (a) If "yes," let's have a closer look => to dos: (1) clearly delineate the tested transaction (closely linked transactions will be difficult to evaluate with a CUP)[14] , (2) evaluate a broad range of relevant comparability factors, (3) perform adjustment calculations, and (4) observe Step 3a, especially if you are not 100% convinced of the reliability of your adjustment calculations

[14]Remember one of the lessons from the case study in Sect. 2.2: Often (esp. when involving one party with a limited functional profile) transactions are so closely linked and of continuous nature that they cannot be evaluated adequately on a separate basis (OECD Guidelines, Paragraph 3.9). As emphasized above, an aggregated analysis will often reduce your workload and at the same time provide more reliable results—hence, always check whether aggregation is feasible.

(b) If "no," don't worry => to dos: (1) you may want to summarize your reasons for rejecting the CUP for documentation purposes (see above), and (2) observe Step 3b.

3. Can we apply the CUP as a secondary method?

   (a) If "yes", try to make it work and adopt a flexible approach (in line with OECD-GL, Paragraph 2.17) => to dos: (1) if you are applying an internal CUP, please double- and triple-check your adjustment calculations—how reliable are they really[15]? (2) Re-visit your functional and risk analysis—can you identify a tested party for which an alternative method can be reliably applied? (3) Compare your results from the CUP to the results obtained from applying an alternative method (3a) if the results match/overlap you can relax (3b) if the results do not match you need to investigate the reasons (a good guess and starting-point for such analysis would be that the assumed CUP is not so good after all).
   (b) If "no," about time: Move on => to do: find a more reliable method.

Case Study: Applying the CUP for Intercompany Transactions of the Prima Group

So, let's not get too creative at this point. What you should remember from the previous case studies is that (1) based on their functional profile, the subsidiaries of Prima have been classified as routine entities and (2) the transactions between Prima and the subsidiaries are so closely linked and of continuous nature that they cannot be evaluated adequately on a separate basis.

Looking at the CUP decision tree, we can proceed as follows:

1. The Prima household electronics do not constitute a commodities transaction, and we can **confidently rule out an external CUP**. Obviously a "quoted price" does not exist. Prima also constitutes a unique brand, and it will be virtually impossible to adjust for brand value when comparing Prima products to other branded household products (remember how strictly the comparability criteria are interpreted by the OECD in the context of a CUP). Also, just imagine that you were in charge of transfer pricing for the PlayStation Division of Sony,[16] would

[15] Again, you should be careful. While the first impulse of the sales organization is often "we do not systematically discriminate in our pricing between subsidiaries and independent sales partners," you will, when taking a closer look, often find that the transactions differ rather substantially—i.e., when looking at issues such as exclusivity and product portfolio of the distributors as well as the range of supportive functions that are intertwined with the sales transaction (see previous footnote). An illustration is provided by the case study in the sub-section for applying the resale price method.

[16] I have no idea about the transfer pricing of Sony. But as an enthusiastic consumer of that particular Sony product, I can assure you that a PlayStation and a Xbox are completely different products and a CUP would make no sense whatsoever (that rationale is, perhaps, even more compelling when thinking about the Nintendo Wii). Naturally, that doesn't imply that Sony would not look at Microsoft when making pricing decisions, but it is conceptually unsound, from a tax as well as a business perspective, to use these prices as an orientation (let alone substitute) for your transfer prices.

you determine your transfer prices based on Xbox prices you observe on the market?

2. An internal CUP will also be difficult to apply for the sale of Prima products. While it is absolutely conceivable that there are markets in which Prima also sells to independent distributors or agents, the functional profile (business strategies) of these independent partners will almost certainly differ from those of the Prima subsidiaries. These differences will also be reflected in the differences between conditions agreed between Prima and independent agents compared to those stipulated in the Sales and Cooperation Agreement with the subsidiaries. There will also be a host of additional comparability factors (i.e., sales volume, payment terms, etc.) for which adjustment calculations would have to be performed. Lastly, and most importantly, the closely linked and continuous nature of the transactions between Prima and the subsidiaries must not be forgotten. Thus, **in sum, an internal CUP does not seem to qualify as the most reliable method to apply to the tested transaction**
3. Despite the limitations identified above, and here comes the curious aspect of the CUP, it would still be advisable to at least look at the "discarded CUPs." While we will find more appropriate methods to ensure that the subsidiaries (tested parties) receive an arm's length remuneration, the CUP can still be of relevance for adding "plausibility" to the arm's length nature of the transfer prices—either as a secondary method or as a kind of an "additional negotiation chip" in the "bargaining game" with tax authorities. For now, however, we can confidently move on to the next method.

Box 3.1 Restating the Lesson

Comparing "Like with Like" Is No Trivial Task

It makes economic and business sense to look at available market prices for comparable products when making pricing decisions. To ensure that the identified prices are a sensible reference point, however, you need to assess whether the products or services are indeed comparable to those exchanged with a related party and whether the economic circumstances of your controlled transactions are likely to have distorting effects. When you conduct this analysis in a diligent manner, you will sometimes succeed in establishing a viable middle ground between the tax and management perspective. In many cases, however, you will have to accept that no adequately comparable price can be identified and that you need to look for alternative methods which are more likely to yield a reliable approximation of an arm's length price. Do not shrug of deficits in comparability when thinking about applying a CUP. Small differences in the nature of the products or the economic circumstances can have immediate and substantial effects on the price. When you fail to identify and adjust for those differences, chances are that your (transfer) prices deviate

(continued)

Box 3.1 (continued)
from arm's length conditions in a "big" rather than a "marginal" way [pun intended].

Obviously, there is nothing artificial or sinister about not applying a CUP. It also does not imply that the arm's length principle is inherently flawed. Pricing decisions are complex and cannot always be reduced to looking at a quoted price. Any manager will tell you that you need to consider the entire value creation process and the (currently prevailing) economic circumstances when setting your price—otherwise you will either sell too cheap or price yourself out of the market.

Now, within MNE, the disciplinary effects of the market are absent. Hence, adopting market prices based on an incomplete understanding of "comparability" may be sustainable for a long period of time. It is even likely that most people feel confident to act in accordance with the arm's length principle in such a case. Alas, they harbor a delusion. And, more importantly, it is likely that the pricing structure is uncompetitive; i.e., it facilitates a suboptimal incentive structure. The bottom line is that an unreliable CUP translates into substantial tax risks and that you should not apply the CUP without taking the issue of comparability to heart.

Based on an appropriate understanding of the CUP and the issue of comparability, it should also be evident that any "tax gap" estimates that are calculated based on price (custom declarations) between controlled and uncontrolled transactions are economic nonsense—at least if these figures are presented and politicized with the intent to "expose" how flawed the arm's length principle is. These propagators pursue a hostile agenda. They basically accuse all MNEs of abusing transfer pricing to avoid taxes and suggest adopting formulary apportionment instead. We, as transfer pricing professionals, should engage in the respective discourse and point out that respective tax gap estimates are based on an incomplete understanding of the arm's length principle—and, ultimately, are just bad economics.

3.2 The Resale Price Method

The resale price method (RPM) is a rather popular method for the sale of products within an MNE (see Fig. 3.6). Certainly not coincidentally, it is also a method which tends to greatly minimize the conflicting views of the management accounting perspective and the tax perspective on transfer prices. From the management accounting perspective, the focus on market or end-customer prices is perceived as sensible, including different prices for individual markets (which are essentially price adjustments). From the tax perspective, the focus on the resale price margin provides the opportunity to explicitly link the pricing mechanism to the functional and risk analysis—which, as discussed above, will be the precondition for

OECD Guidelines 2017, Paragraph 2.27

The resale price method begins with the price at which a product that has been purchased from an associated enterprise is **resold to an independent enterprise**. This **price (the resale price) is then reduced by an appropriate gross margin** on this price (the "resale price margin") representing the amount out of which the reseller would seek to cover its selling and other operating expenses and, **in the light of the functions performed** (taking into account assets used and risks assumed), **make an appropriate profit**. [...] This method is probably most useful where it is applied to marketing operations.

Fig. 3.6 Resale price method (source: OECD)

eliminating systemic transfer pricing risks. The following key aspects regarding the RPM must be understood to appreciate why it will often be superior to a CUP:

- It focuses on "functional comparability" rather than on "product comparability," which implies a much less restrictive interpretation of the required degree of comparability. As emphasized by the OECD (Paragraph 2.29): "In making comparisons for purposes of the resale price method, fewer adjustments are normally needed to account for product differences than under the CUP method, because minor product differences are less likely to have as material an effect on profit margins as they do on price". Analogous to the CUP, the RPM can be applied either based on reference to the resale price margin that the same reseller earns on items purchased and sold in comparable uncontrolled transactions ("internal comparable") or based on the resale price margin earned by an independent enterprise in comparable uncontrolled transactions, which may serve as a guide ("external comparable").
- The functional profile of the tested party will be the focal point of the comparability analysis: "In a market economy, the compensation for performing similar functions would tend to be equalized across different activities. [. . .]. Because gross profit margins represent gross compensation, after the cost of sales for specific functions performed [. . .] product differences are less significant."
- The basic relationship between the functional profile and the gross margin, i.e., a more extensive functional profile will ceteris paribus have to be reflected in a higher gross margin, is rather straightforward. As emphasized by the OECD (Paragraph 2.37): "If the reseller in the controlled transaction does not carry on a substantial commercial activity but only transfers the goods to a third party, the resale price margin could, in light of the functions performed, be a small one. The resale price margin could be higher where it can be demonstrated that the reseller has some special expertise in the marketing of such goods, in effect bears special risks, or contributes substantially to the creation or maintenance of intangible property associated with the product."
- It will generally be easier to identify companies that perform similar functions to an internal reseller rather than to identify prices for products that fulfill the restrictive comparability criteria outlined in Sect. 2.1—especially when looking at a tested party with a limited functional profile (as emphasized by the OECD in Paragraph 2.32), of which there is plenty of public data available (see further

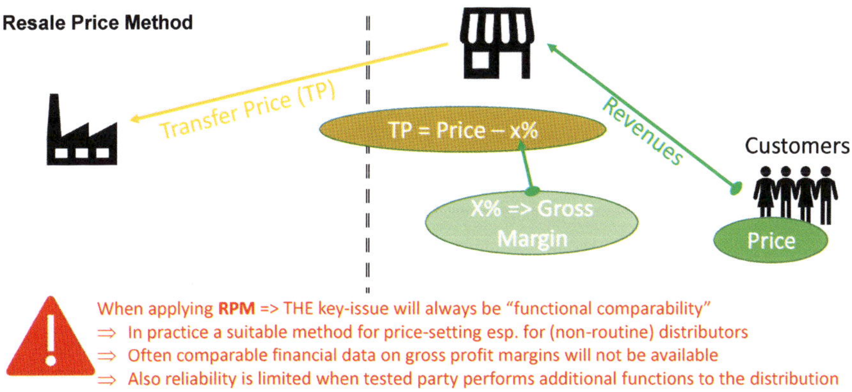

Fig. 3.7 Applying the RPM (Source: own Illustration)

below). Naturally, the reliability of the RPM will decrease if the reseller performs complex (highly value-adding) functions in addition to reselling activities.[17]

Figure 3.7 provides an illustration of the "mechanics" of the RPM.

The OECD emphasizes that "[. . .] where uncontrolled and controlled transactions are comparable in all characteristics other than the product itself, the resale price method might produce a more reliable measure of arm's length conditions than the CUP method, unless reasonably accurate adjustments could be made to account for differences in the products transferred" (Paragraph 2.32). To me, the OECD position on this issue always seemed rather weak. At verbatim, the referenced statement of the OECD is trivial—bordering on being ridiculous. Obviously, the CUP can be applied where reasonably accurate adjustments could be made—but as seen in the previous section, that will be a rare exception and will not provide you with a viable tax position especially not on a stand-alone basis. The stance of the OECD, in the sense that it feels compelled to defend the CUP, is puzzling. There is no sense in dwelling on it, however, as these concerns are largely of theoretical nature, while those at the heart of the limitations of the RPM are of practical nature. The main caveat of applying the RPM is that "[. . .] the level of activity performed by the reseller, whether minimal or substantial, would need to be well supported by relevant evidence" when evaluating the relationship between gross margin and functional profile referred to above (i.e., OECD-GL Paragraph 2.37).[18] How will you demonstrate the "special expertise" in the marketing of some goods, let alone quantify appropriate adjustments to the gross margin? Well, the answer, as always, is that it depends on the specific facts and circumstances of the case. A more general answer

[17]While the OECD is correct (consistent) in pointing out these limitations, the respective guidelines should clarify that the CUP will be even less reliable in respective circumstances (the current wording of Paragraph 2.32 could be interpreted to imply the opposite).

[18]One may consider this to be a "fun fact," but this is actually the only time that the OECD uses the phrase "well supported" throughout the entire OECD-GL.

that will be valuable in your day-to-day work is that you need to critically evaluate whether the RPM can be regarded as a reliable method on a stand-alone basis. In most cases, the answer will be negative, and you will find that combining the RPM with a secondary method (in 90% of the cases the TNMM) will offer an advantageous trade-off.

Hence, when evaluating the possible application of the RPM with your colleagues/clients, the following points may provide a sensible basis for your discussion (the "**RPM decision tree**"):

1. Have we excluded the applicability of a CUP?

   (a) If "yes," great => you may want to document your reasons for rejecting the CUP, i.e., it is not feasible to conduct sufficiently reliable adjustments—in this context, the stipulations of OECD-GL in Paragraph 2.32 are to be observed.
   (b) If "no" or you were "unsure" => collect the data required for the CUP and archive it. Once the comparability based on the RPM is concluded, you can check whether the CUP can be utilized as a secondary method (see also case study in Sect. 3.1 as well as the advanced sections).

2. Can we identify a tested party exhibiting a limited (routine) functional and risk profile?

   (a) If "yes," we already know that the tested party is not expected to share in the residual profits and should generally exhibit small but comparable stable profits.[19] These can, generally, be substantiated by looking at the net margins of comparable companies, i.e., applying the so-called "modified RPM" or "TNMM"—see Sect. 3.3. This will always tend to be the "easier" path in this context and one of the main reasons why you should always aim at establishing an unambiguous classification of the transacting parties.
   (b) If "no," you will have to substantiate the economic activity of the tested party (distributor) in a much more detail; i.e., compared to the path illustrated in 2a, there is no predefined expectation to guide your analysis. Once you classify the distributor as a nonroutine entity (or you apply labels such as "fully-fledged distributor"—see above), the share of the distributor in the residual profit (loss) essentially will depend on the value contributions relative to the other (non-tested) party (i.e., an entrepreneur exhibiting only a slightly more pronounced functional profile compared to the tested party[20]). Hence, the results of the tested party will be much more volatile in such cases.

---

[19] Some countries, including Germany, have actually explicitly integrated the expectations of small but stable profits into their transfer pricing regulations (Paragraph 3.4.10.2. a of the administrative principles procedure—"Verwaltungsgrundsätze-Verfahren").

[20] Note: The situation must be conceived as such, i.e., there should still be a transacting party acting as an entrepreneur and exhibiting a more pronounced functional profile; if this were not the case, a tested party could not be identified and (most likely) a one-sided transfer pricing method would not be applicable. Instead, especially when the transaction parties interact in a closely integrated value

3. Can we identify sufficiently reliable data for the comparability analysis?
   (a) If "yes," you will have to provide a detailed documentation on the performed adjustment calculation—this applies for internal as well as for external comparables (see above). Due to the lack of publicly available data on gross margins in commercial databases (as acknowledged by the OECD, see OECD-GL, Paragraph 2.4), however, the RPM will in most cases only be applicable based on "internal comparables" which tend to be readily available. In this context, similar to the CUP, the taxpayer cannot afford to neglect to consider how restrictive the comparability criteria tend to be applied. The example provided by the OECD (see OECD-GL, Paragraph 2.44) accurately describes a situation often encountered in practice, i.e., an MNE that sells its product through independent distributors in some (fringe) markets but has established a subsidiary for the sales in a core market. As functional differences will immediately impact the gross margin, you will have to adjust for a wide range of differences, some of which are easy to quantify (i.e., inventory levels or costs for warranty services) and some of which are near impossible to quantify (exclusive distribution rights, technical services, management efficiency[21]).
   (b) If "no," you can almost consider yourself lucky. As just explained, however, internal comparables will often be available for the purpose of applying the RPM. You should carefully outline that performing the required adjustments is not feasible for the controlled transaction—at least not in a sufficiently reliable manner.[22]

When discussing the RPM, one note should be made in respect to transfer prices based on "commissions." MNEs often utilize turnover-based commissions for managing (incentivizing) their sales network—including independent distributors as well as subsidiaries that perform sales functions. In economic terms, a commission is equivalent to a gross margin, and commission-based pricing can thus be best understood as a subtype of the RPM. There tends to be one twist, however, and that relates primarily to the functional and risk analysis (Step 2a. of our RPM

---

chain, the profit split method would offer a better fit—and/or tax authorities would be prone to make respective challenges—see also decision tree for the profit split method below.

[21] The need to account (adjust) for the effect of management efficiency sounds almost esoteric, but it is explicitly stated in Paragraph 2.33 of the OECD-GL. Ultimately, you can only strive to substantiate that the degree of comparability is considered adequate—compiling detailed documentation (proactively outlining your arguments) will carry you a long way, while being unprepared or careless in respect to comparability adjustments when applying the RPM is a recipe for disaster.

[22] In other words—in case you are faced with a situation in which internal comparables are deemed unreliable (or disadvantageous), use a reference to the strict comparability criteria in your favor, i.e., to substantiate your choice of the modified RPM or TNMM as the best available method.

decision tree[23]). In day-to-day practice, most internal sales entities that are remunerated based on commission tend to exhibit a rather limited functional and risk profile. The financial results realized by these entities will, however, tend to be rather volatile (i.e., seeing operating margins fluctuating between –20 and +20% in an MNE's sales organization is not an exotic exception[24]) which is difficult to align with the default expectation of small but stable profits for routine entities. Your first priority in such a case should be to substantiate the routine classification and explore options with the management accounting team to limit the erratic nature of the operating margins, i.e., some sort of (year-end) adjustment procedure—as discussed in Sect. 3.3—would be recommended but is sometimes difficult to implement (vetoed) as it is perceived to eliminate the incentivizing effect of the commissions. The second, more technical, caveat with respect to commissions relates to the comparability analysis (specifically to the choice of an appropriate profit level indicator ("PLI"). As commissionaires only facilitate the sales on behalf of their principal without assuming ownership of the product, the profit and loss statement of a commissionaire differs substantially from that of a re-seller (limited risk or fully fledged) that actually purchases the products before reselling (sometimes with a substantial time gap) and whose P&L thus reflects the respective material costs and (real) revenues related to the sale of the products (instead of commissions earned). Hence, you should be careful to avoid comparing "apples" and "oranges"—the quantitative effects will be illustrated below.

Case Study: Applying the RPM for Intercompany Transactions of the Prima Group

Again, let's not get too creative at this point. We have firmly established that (1) based on their functional profile, the subsidiaries of Prima GmbH are adequately classified as routine entities and (2) the transactions between Prima and the subsidiaries can be evaluated on an aggregated basis.

Looking at the RPM decision tree, we can proceed as follows:

1. The Prima household electronics do not exhibit features of a commodities transaction and we were reasonably confident in ruling out an external CUP. Based on the information provided in Sect. 2.1, however, we need to consider that the price-setting within the Prima Group is based on a Master Price List ("MPL") and country-specific discounts or rebate (as well as commission) rates. In such a case, it is imperative to ask whether internal comparables can be identified. As indicated in the case study for the CUP, it is conceivable that there are markets in which Prima also sells to independent distributors. While the degree of comparability of these transactions was (swiftly) discarded as being insufficient for

[23]Note: The problems outlined in Step 2b of the RPM decision tree can also be exacerbated in the case of commissions.

[24]Note: Such "erratic" results for entities with a comparatively homogeneous (limited) functional profile are inviting disaster (i.e., raising the suspicions of the tax auditor and opening the door for painful (and hard to defend against) transfer pricing adjustments).

applying the CUP, we need to be more careful when dealing with the RPM, as the comparability threshold is focused on "functional comparability" and generally interpreted in less restrictive terms. Let's assume our question with respect to internal comparables would be answered by the company representatives as follows (which would be a somewhat typical answer):

"Yes:

- We have two independent agents in Russia and Australia
- Our subsidiary in the USA used to be an independent agent until it was bought by Prima three years ago
- Our sales subsidiaries are in core markets for Prima, i.e. currently UK, Italy, Spain and the Netherlands
- Since last year we have also established subsidiaries in Denmark (for Northern Europe) and in Hungary (for CEE Region) to explore these new markets."

2. Based on the functional and risk analysis (see Sect. 2.2), the Prima sales subsidiaries can reliably be classified as routine entities and thus constitute an uncontested choice as tested party. It will generally prove feasible to identify sufficiently comparable companies in commercial databases, i.e., "functionally comparable" distributors operating in the same industry and geographic region as the Prima subsidiaries. Considering that the routine classification provides us with a clearly defined expectation in terms of an arm's length profit allocation (i.e., small but stable profits for the tested party), we will likely find ourselves pursuing Step 2.a. of the RPM decision tree—in combination with subsequently applying Step 3.b. (i.e., applying the modified RPM or TNMM which will be demonstrated in Sect. 3.3).[25]

   Considering the relevant facts and circumstances for the case at hand, however, we should not take a respective shortcut just yet. Specifically, two factors should be considered. *First*, looking back at the functional and risk analysis, we need to realize that some ambiguities remain, i.e., a lack of delineation between marketing and service function as well as an uncertainty regarding the extent of the market risk borne by the subsidiaries (remember the "Achilles Heel" identified earlier)—i.e., in sum the functional profile does not resemble that of a "bare bones" routine entity. *Second*, considering that it was brought to our attention that Prima undertakes transactions with independent third parties (sales agents in Russia and Australia), we need to analyze whether these third parties can reasonably be considered as functionally comparable and could thus be utilized as

[25]An important aspect that, in day-to-day practice, would tilt the scale toward choosing the TNMM rather than the RPM is the level of aggregation adopted for the analysis; i.e., as outlined above, it is sensible to integrate the analysis of the arm's length pricing for the centralized services rendered by the Prima GmbH in the analysis for the remuneration of local subsidiaries (tested parties) for their performance of the sales activities—a respective aggregation will, however, not be feasible when applying the RPM which would require either a segmented analysis or adjustment calculations to ensure an adequate degree of comparability of the gross margins or commission rates—see also below.

internal comparables.[26] Hence, we will, in a first step, carefully walk through Step 2.b. (*classification and "functional comparability"*) and Step 3.a. ("available data for the comparability analysis").

To determine whether the independent agents selling Prima products in Russia and Australia can be considered as being sufficiently comparable to the Prima subsidiaries, we can obviously conduct a functional and risks analysis. Let's assume for the sake of this case study, as is often the case in practice, that the independent agents do merely provide rudimentary first-level support and do not perform any marketing activities specifically targeted at promoting the Prima brand. In terms of functional comparability, if considered on a stand-alone basis, these differences could arguably be considered not to be so severe as to outright reject comparability in the context of applying the RPM—it would, however, also be recommended to revisit the assumption that all Prima subsidiaries exhibit homogeneous functional profiles (i.e., it could be assumed that the functional profile of the newly established subsidiaries in the smaller markets is more limited compared to that of the established subsidiaries operating in core markets).[27] Also, while the contractual provisions of the agreements concluded with the independent agents might be similar to those concluded with the subsidiaries (i.e., regarding the applicable MPL or the agreed commission rate), other relevant comparability factors might render the comparison to be unfeasible. Important respective factors often bearing relevance in practice, which are also assumed to apply to the case study, are differences in the business strategy (including exclusivity of brands and the product portfolio or supplementary business activities) of the independent agents as well as the (relative) volume of their purchases. For the sake of our case study, it is reasonable to assume that the share of revenues related to the distribution of Prima products is much smaller for the independent agents (i.e., below 20%) compared to that of the local subsidiaries which exclusively distribute Prima products. Another reasonable assumption would be that the business activities of the independent agent in Russia are not solely focused on the distribution of (selective and high-end) household electronics but that it rather has a second business unit focused on distributing other luxury goods and that the agent is solely operating in Moscow (i.e., the business strategy of the agent is to select only the very-high-end products of the Prima product range).

An interesting, nonstandard, element of the case at hand is the subsidiary in the USA. Here, it would be most interesting to investigate whether the conditions previously agreed (i.e., while the company was still an independent agent) have been sustained upon integrating the company into the Prima Group or whether the

[26]Note: In such a situation, you can generally bet the farm on the tax authorities making detailed respective inquiries. Hence, even in case you have concluded that the TNMM is the most reliable method, you should "cover all the bases" to put yourself in a favorable position in case of a tax audit.

[27]When encountering a respective case in practice, it would be strongly recommended to conduct a more detailed functional and risk analysis to get a more specific idea of the scope of differences.

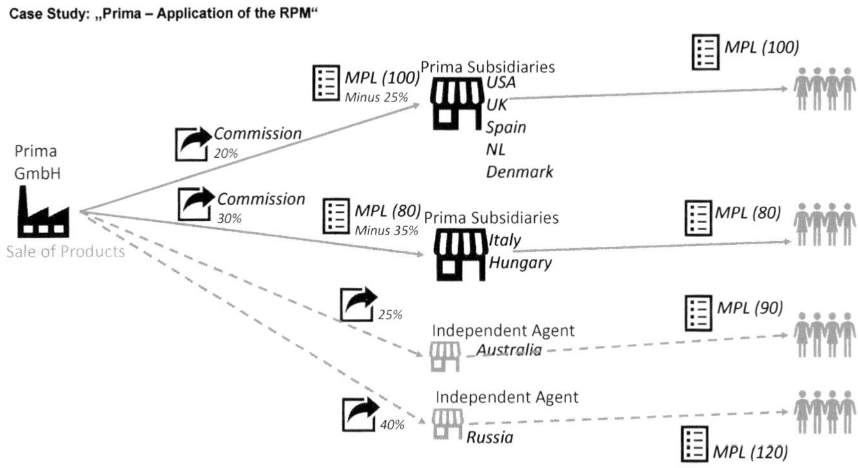

Fig. 3.8 Price-setting of the Prima Group (Source: own illustration)

pricing has been modified and what the rationale of the modifications was. Let's assume, for the sake of the case study, that the previously independent agent maintained a very close relationship with Prima (i.e., 80% of the revenues were related to Prima products, and the service personnel had received some training by Prima to provide first- as well as second-level support to local customers). It can therefore be reasonably assumed that the economic situations were not drastically altered upon integrating the agent into the Prima Group and that the agreed pricing has indeed been maintained.

Figure 3.8 summarizes and specifies the applied discounts from the MPL and commission rates within the Prima Group.

As illustrated above, the Prima MPL differentiates according to local market conditions. The MPL is applied vis-à-vis the end customer and thus directly reflects arm's length conditions; i.e., it is exclusively driven by management of accounting considerations aimed at increasing the profits of the Prima Group rather than transfer pricing or tax-related considerations (i.e., it is assumed that the allocation of profits among group entities does not impact the price-setting). But what conclusions regarding the compliance with the arm's length principle can we deduce from comparing the commission rates negotiated with the independent agents with the transfer prices agreed between Prima and its local subsidiaries? Well, unfortunately, we cannot conclude much. Some viable, albeit highly tentative, conclusions could be:

- The commission rates negotiated with the independent agents "do not differ drastically" from those agreed between Prima and the local subsidiaries—i.e., the commission rate for the independent agent in Australia reflects the median between the 20% rate agreed with the subsidiaries on the core markets and the 30% agreed with the subsidiaries in the fringe markets

  - The higher commission rate agreed with the local subsidiaries could be justified in case difficult market conditions can be substantiated (i.e., at the end of the day, this will boil down to looking at the net margins of the subsidiaries—see below)
  - In a German tax audit, the fact that the commission rates were in agreement with the subsidiaries located in the core markets are lower than those agreed with independent agents would provide a certain level of comfort and a favorable starting-position; i.e., it would be sensible to emphasize the favorable price-setting when compiling the transfer pricing documentation for Germany[28] => the flip-side here is that this will be mirrored by a more difficult initial position in the countries in which the local subsidiaries are located.
  - The rate agreed with the independent agent in Russia is likely attributable to the idiosyncratic conditions prevailing on the local market (as well as the business strategy pursued by that specific agent). Here it will most likely be helpful to reject comparability and exclude this agent as an internal comparable.

- With respect to the resale margin, we can conclude that the gross margin is (slightly) higher compared to the commission rate (i.e., 25–20% for the core markets and 35–30% for the fringe markets). Considering that the functional analysis did not yield any substantial differences between the commission and the resale business, the comparable small differential in the gross margin seems somewhat plausible (i.e., reflecting an additional compensation for the risks assumed by the resellers regarding inventory (obsolesce) as well as (possibly) risks relating to warrant and exchange rates.[29] Hence, by imputation, we could make the argument that since the commission rates are not disadvantageous from the perspective of the Prima GmbH, the agreed resale (gross) margins are also to be considered in line with market conditions.
- For the transfer prices agreed with Prima USA, however, the relevant facts and circumstances are more beneficial. To be sure, we would have to substantiate that the main parameters of the transaction (volume, contractual obligation, scope of services) remained material unchanged and that the time gap is unlikely to distort

[28]Whether this tentative conclusion is viable would, in the context of the case study, heavily depend on the scale of the centralized services rendered by the Prima GmbH. A higher scope of services (i.e., additional functions and related costs at the level of Prima GmbH) would ceteris paribus require a lower commission rate compared to a business relationship in which Prima GmbH does not render centralized services (as would be assumed for the transactions with the independent sales agents).

[29]Again, the inevitable drawbacks of a somewhat rudimentary functional and risk analysis are exposed here. Without having a more specific idea of how the risks are allocated between the parties, it will be difficult to quantify (approximate) the likely effect on the gross margin. When you encounter a case in which you need to deal with the applicability of the RPM (i.e., ambiguous functional profile or availability of internal comparables), you will need to revisit the functional analysis and clarify these issues.

the analysis. But ultimately, it is likely that a commission rate of 20% that was agreed with an independent agent 3 years ago will continue to appropriately reflect arm's length conditions and can be utilized as a transfer price. Two caveats need to be kept in mind. *First*, we will need to ascertain that the functions and especially the risks of the distributor remained (largely) unchanged. *Second*, it will not be feasible to infer from the agreement for the USA that a 20% commission reflect arm's length conditions on the other markets.

- What about external comparables—can we substantiate the tentative conclusions derived from the internal comparables by making a reference to external comparables? As pointed out in Step 3a of our RPM decision tree, publicly available data on gross margin is scarce. Some data on sales commission, however, is publicly available. A respective source that used to be cited in the transfer pricing literature is the so-called "MANA Survey of Sales Commissions" from 2003.[30] The survey contains information on commission rates according to the type of products (differentiating between 134 types) sold as well as the category of sales (i.e., sales to end-users, OEMs, or distributors). For Prima, the category "Electronic Consumer Products" arguably constitutes the best fit of the available categories, yielding a range of commission rates from 7.50% (highest) to 3.50% (lowest) with an average of 5.50%.[31] At first glance, these rates seem to indicate that the commission rates agreed between Prima GmbH and the local subsidiaries are uncharacteristically high and could indicate a deviation from arm's length conditions—such a conclusion would, however, be grossly misleading—as evidenced by the agreements with third parties. If anything, this brief example should make you cautious about basing your comparability analysis on public references when comparing gross margins (at least on a stand-alone basis). As will be shown below, there are publicly available references that can be utilized when applying the TNMM (or C+, see below)—but when applying the RPM, you should generally stay away from such references.[32]

Now, in the beginning of this book, I have said that one should embrace the concept "transfer pricing is not an exact science." But, when we are completely honest with ourselves, an analysis as the one outlined above will not be enough, even when applying an explicitly magnanimous interpretation of the arm's length principle. Or would you feel comfortable entering a tax audit with nothing in your hand but these tentative conclusions? The shortcoming of the analysis based on the RPM will,

[30]The survey was published by the Manufacturers' Agents National Association in the *Agency Sales* magazine in October 2003.

[31]Here you can already glean one caveat of the MANA survey—the data is not nearly as comprehensive as the set-up of the survey suggests; i.e., while it covers 134 product types, it is merely based on a total number of 1021 respondents. For the "Electronic Consumer Products," it seems likely that the data merely comprises two responses (7.50 and 3.50%).

[32]If you do have access to industry-specific data on gross margins or commission that may not be (easily) available to the public, it might be feasible utilize these as external comparables for transfer pricing purposes—but you should be aware of the risks exemplified in the case study and proceed with appropriate care.

Prima USA	2016	2017	2018	Total	Average
Revenues	5,000,000 €	5,500,000 €	6,000,000 €	16,500,000 €	5,500,000 €
COGS	3,000,000 €	3,200,000 €	3,400,000 €	9,600,000 €	3,200,000 €
Gross Margin (%)	40.0%	41.8%	43.3%	41.8%	41.8%
OPEX	1,500,000 €	1,800,000 €	2,500,000 €	5,800,000 €	1,933,333 €
EBIT	500,000 €	500,000 €	100,000 €	1,100,000 €	366,667 €
Net Margin (%)	10.0%	9.1%	1.7%	6.7%	6.7%

Fig. 3.9 P&L Prima USA (source: own Illustration)

Prima UK	2016	2017	2018	Total	Average
Revenues	6,000,000 €	5,500,000 €	6,800,000 €	18,300,000 €	6,100,000 €
COGS	4,800,000 €	4,400,000 €	5,000,000 €	14,200,000 €	4,733,333 €
Gross Margin (%)	20.0%	20.0%	26.5%	22.4%	22.4%
OPEX	1,500,000 €	1,300,000 €	1,400,000 €	4,200,000 €	1,400,000 €
EBIT	(–) 300,000 €	(–) 200,000 €	600,000 €	100,000 €	33,333 €
Net Margin (%)	–5.0%	–3.6%	8.8%	0.5%	0.5%

Fig. 3.10 P&L Prima UK (source: own Illustration)

Prima Spain	2016	2017	2018	Total	Average
Revenues	4,000,000 €	4,500,000 €	4,000,000 €	12,500,000 €	4,166,667 €
COGS	2,800,000 €	3,200,000 €	2,900,000 €	8,900,000 €	2,966,667 €
Gross Margin (%)	30.0%	28.9%	27.5%	28.8%	28.8%
OPEX	1,300,000 €	1,400,000 €	1,400,000 €	4,100,000 €	1,366,667 €
EBIT	–100,000 €	–100,000 €	–300,000 €	–500,000 €	–166,667 €
Net Margin (%)	–2.5%	–2.2%	–7.5%	–4.0%	–4.0%

Fig. 3.11 P&L Prima Spain (source: own Illustration)

however, only become fully apparent when looking at the net margins of the local subsidiaries. There is a pretty good chance that, based on the arc of the story outlined above, you would find the P&L statements of the subsidiaries to look something like those shown in Figs. 3.9, 3.10, 3.11, and 3.12.[33]

The first and most important aspect to notice is that the net margins are not aligned with the generalized "expectations" for routine entities, i.e., small but stable profits on a continuous basis. Except for Prima USA, all local entities realized

[33] To keep the presentation concise, let us limit the analysis to four selected subsidiaries.

Prima Hungary	2016	2017	2018	Total	Average
Revenues	1,000,000 €	1,500,000 €	2,500,000 €	5,000,000 €	1,666,667 €
COGS	600,000 €	900,000 €	1,500,000 €	3,000,000 €	1,000,000 €
Gross Margin (%)	40.0%	40.0%	40.0%	40.0%	40.0%
OPEX	600,000 €	700,000 €	700,000 €	2,000,000 €	666,667 €
EBIT	(–) 200.000 €	(–) 100,000 €	300,000 €	0 €	0 €
Net Margin (%)	–20,0%	–6.7%	12.0%	0.0%	0.0%

Fig. 3.12 P&L Prima Hungary (source: own Illustration)

("suffered") losses in at least one fiscal year. This constitutes a clandestine "red flag," and it would be our immediate task to analyze the reasons for the losses. As, arguably quite sensibly, pointed out by the OECD, "[w]hen an associated enterprise consistently realizes losses while the MNE group as a whole is profitable, the facts could trigger some special scrutiny of transfer pricing issue" (OECD-GL 2017a, Paragraph 1.129).

Neglecting to address this task will generally translate into severe transfer pricing risks, as the tax authorities dealing with a local routine entity in a loss position will almost certainly jump at the opportunity to challenge the arm's length nature of the transfer prices; i.e., from their perspective, the prices charged to the local subsidiary must have been too high (i.e., the resale margin or commission was set too low), and they will aim to adjust the prices in a way that aligns the net margins of the local distributor with the expectation of the tax authorities—should you face an aggressive auditor, he could, as a "first offer" type of assessment, propose an adjustment to 10% (perhaps claiming that this would be a profit level commonly realized by local distributors operating in the same industry[34]). Now, that does not necessarily imply that you would have to accept such an adjustment as various defensive strategies (see below) will be feasible, but you have certainly gotten a bad start into your tax audit—having created a sense of "entitlement" and the prospect of a "quick-win" for the tax authorities. In other words, having based your transfer pricing solely on the RPM will often make it more likely that you will have to fight an uphill battle.

Now, let's briefly look at some of the defensive strategies that could be utilized by Prima in the case at hand—focusing on aspects highlighted by the OECD (the list, obviously, is not exhaustive):

- As emphasized by the OECD (OECD-RL, Paragraph 1.129): "Of course, associated enterprises, like independent enterprises, can sustain **genuine losses**, whether due to heavy start-up costs, unfavourable economic conditions, inefficiencies, or other **legitimate business** reasons". In the case of Prima, but essentially in each other case involving losses, we will try to build on this emphasis as

[34]Such claim could be made on the basis of either so-called secret comparables or even a benchmark study performed by the authorities (applying TNMM).

much as possible. For Prima Hungary, the financial data clearly reflect that the local distributor was progressing through a start-up phase in the period 2016–2018 (i.e., the revenues doubled from 2016 to 2018). Pursuant to the OECD (OECD-RL, Paragraph 1.131): "Recurring losses for **a reasonable period** may be justified in some cases by a business strategy to [. . .] achieve market penetration". Considering that Prima Hungary realized profits in 2018 that "compensate" the losses incurred in 2016 and 2017, there should be a rather sound case here for arguing that the losses were attributable to legitimate business reasons and did not exceed a reasonable period.

- A similar argument could be made to defend the losses realized by the UK entity in 2016 and 2017, i.e., here it seems to be a contraction of the business in 2016 and 2017 which will conceivably be linked to legitimate business reasons. It is, however, less evident that the profits realized in 2018 would be considered "sufficient" compensation for losses realized in the previous business yeas; i.e., Prima UK is not progressing through a start-up phase, and the level of profitability would therefore be expected to approximate the profit level of "comparable companies" when considering a multiple-year period.[35]
- Given the (limited) facts and circumstances of the case at hand, it will be rather challenging to defend the continuous losses suffered by Prima Spain—demonstrating the adverse economic conditions persisting on the local market and explaining other legitimate business reasons will usually require substantial effort and will only be suitable to mitigate the risks, there is no chance of eliminating the risks.[36]

In the case at hand, defending the losses will generally be more challenging, the more the functional profiles of the local distributors are geared toward a "bare bones routine" classification. While routine entities are, as a general rule, not isolated from market risks, the extent to which they bear respective risks must be limited—in line with the "expectations" formulated above. In the case at hand, you could, at least to a certain extent, exploit the "ambiguities" of the existing functional and risk analysis, but you would have to proceed with great caution, i.e., (1) you should never undermine the consistency of your transfer pricing documentation, (2) you need to be aware that this will make it much harder to build the TNMM into your arguments, and (3) there is a "path dependency" in the sense that if you justify (larger) losses based on a more extensive functional and risk profile today, you will have to stomach the demands of compensating (larger) profits in the future (in our case this could apply to Prima UK).

[35]More details on the advantages of a multiple-year analysis below. Undoubtedly, you start to realize by now that there is no escaping the analysis and discussion of the net margins—please bear with me though.

[36]Again, some additional options might be available in the context of the TNMM—i.e., specifically, including loss-making local comparables in a respective benchmarking analysis pursuant to OECD-GL, Paragraphs 3.64 and 3.65.

Looking back at the headquarters, i.e., Prima GmbH, the situation does not appear particularly challenging. The financial results (note: at the level of net margins, not the gross margins) of the local distributors show that the agreed resale margins and commission rates are to be viewed as rather "favorable" from a German perspective. The exception to this is the USA. While the net margin (i.e., 10% in 2016 and 9.1% in 2017) is not excessive, it will most likely fall outside of some of the (inter-quartile) arm's length ranges that the tax authorities are familiar with—hence, a respective challenge (i.e., claiming that the profitability of Prima exceeds the profitability of comparable routine distributors in the context of arm's length transactions) would not be completely surprising.[37] The immediate defense against these claims would be to argue that a multiple-year average should be considered as the relevant indicator, as such an approach would eliminate, or at least mitigate, cyclical and other idiosyncratic effects (including accounting-related issue). A respective approach is generally commensurate with the guidance provided by the OECD (OECD-GL, Paragraph 3.77) and makes a great deal of economic sense—at least from the perspective of the tax authorities timing considerations should be of a clearly subordinated nature as their tax base will hardly be systematically be eroded by such effects[38]—further details are discussed below.

In analyzing the financial data above, you may also have noticed that the gross margin (Revenue minus COGS) does not match the resale margin agreed between Prima GmbH and the local subsidiaries (Yes, I know, that was deliberate!). The reason for this is the commission business, for which only the earned commissions will be counted as revenues, whereas no corresponding COGS will be booked in the P&L. As cautioned above, you should be careful to avoid comparing "apples" and "oranges." Taking the example of Prima USA, we can calculate, if the resale margin of 25% was consistently applied, that €4,000,000 of revenue was related to the resale business, while €1,000,000 was earned in commissions (reflecting revenues for Prima GmbH of €5,000,000). Hence for Prima USA, the commission business accounted for about 56% of the business (adjusted revenues).[39] While this is not

[37]What you should also be aware of in this specific context is the impact of the aggregated analysis that was utilized to substantiate the arm's length nature of the prices. Considering that the net margin of the tested party (potentially) falls outside of a range accepted as arm's length, it is no longer feasible to argue that this automatically indicates that the services that were rendered complimentary to the delivery of products were priced at arm's length—the consequence here could be that the tax auditor insists on a segmented analysis (knowing that it will be extremely difficult for the taxpayer to defend the arm's length nature of both transactions on a segmented basis).

[38]In everyday practice, auditions, at least in Germany, tend to be rather stubbornly insisting on timing issues and do not shy away from blatantly ignoring arguments built on multiple-year analysis. While it is to be hoped that the regulatory framework will be amended to provide some additional safeguards to taxpayers against such behavior, you should be careful to always provide a detailed and coherent argument in your transfer pricing documentation to justify the adoption of a multiple-year analysis.

[39]The Prima case study was set up in a way that makes it reasonable to assume that there is no substantial difference regarding the economic circumstances (value contributions) between the

of immediate relevance for Prima in terms of defending the losses incurred by routine entities, being aware of the impact of these accounting issues on the PLI will be of utmost relevance when applying the TNMM[40] (or cost-plus method—see below).

To cut a long story short, the RPM is a sensible transfer pricing method and the obvious choice for setting arm's length prices for the resale business of an MNE. It will, however, require substantial effort in monitoring and adjusting the gross margins (outcome testing) to align the financial results with a profit allocation that is reasonably anticipated based on the functional and risk profile of the reseller (tested party). The key advice here is: Do not be complacent! Do not just stipulate a uniform resale margin and let nature run its course, you will be eaten alive be any tax auditor worth his salt.

Box 3.2 Restating the Lesson
Comparability Does Not Stop at the Gross Margin

The RPM is often intuitively applied, as it is a method that appropriately incentivizes the sales organization and is comparatively easy to implement from a management perspective. However, even management will concede that third parties, when negotiating their commission rates or resale margins, will ultimately have their operating margin in mind. Reminding the management and sales team that they have to consider the (potential) operating margin of the different sales entities when setting their commission rates or resale price margins is not an enviable task (do not expect a "thank you"). Ideally, the ensuing discussion can, however, trigger a worthwhile discussion about different market conditions and optimizing incentive structures. When functionally comparable sales entities operate in different geographic markets that can be identified as tested parties, it is only fair to the local management to adjust

(continued)

resale and the commission business and that therefore, on a net margin level, the comparability analysis is not affected by the differences. In practice, however, you will have to proceed with outmost caution in such a case (i.e., a 50/50 split between two potentially "different" business segments) and a segmented analysis will systematically lead to more tax viable results. You also need to be careful when interpreting the financial data to justify losses (see above; I would argue that neither the conclusions drawn regarding the start-up phase of Prima Hungary nor the conclusions about the economic difficulties faced by Prima UK are materially impacted by the lack of segmentation).

[40] I had to add the disclaimer, as I am walking on thin ice when introducing the working assumption that we do not need to differentiate (segment) between resale and commission business of the tested parties. Naturally, the P&L of a reseller will differ not only in respect to the revenues but also in respect to the working capital (accounts receivable, accounts payable, and inventory). So, when discussing the applicable arm's length margins, you would have to make adjustment calculations to "equalize" the working capital employed of your tested party with those of the comparables. But, in the end of the day, these are "technicalities" (see below) that do not translate into systemic risks. If you caught the need for adjusting for the revenues, you are doing just fine.

Box 3.2 (continued)
the gross margins. You want to reward good sales performance. Hence, the results of the sales entity should depend on the ability to generate sales and keep costs under control. Any external effects that cannot be influenced by the sales entity should be eliminated as far as possible. Failing to appropriately calibrate the gross margins will discourage sales managers in challenging markets and induce complacency in comparatively "soft" markets.

Depending on the complexity of the sales functions performed by the sales entity, the arm's length profit margins may vary considerably. The profitability (losses) will, however, always be "limited" by the total value-added contributions of the sales functions. In case the sales entity contributes unique and valuable intangibles, it cannot be reliably identified as tested party and the RPM will likely not constitute the most appropriate transfer pricing method. While the RPM can certainly be applied for entities exhibiting a functional profile that exceeds a routine classification, you should thus always picture a "virtual limit" or a "soft ceiling" on the profits (losses) of the tested party.

The effects of neglecting to adjust the gross margin to the specific economic circumstances are similar to those resulting for neglecting to adjust the price when applying a CUP. While gross margins are quite sensitive to differences between the controlled transaction and the comparables, the level of sensitivity tends to be smaller compared to the CUP.

Applying the arm's length principle from a tax perspective by emphasizing that the gross margin needs to be adjusted (calibrated) to fit the specific economic circumstances is hardly an artificial or economically dubious position. Quite the opposite, it forces management to diligently analyze market conditions. If you want to be really enthusiastic about it, you may conclude that the arm's length principle does clearly not facilitate aggressive tax structuring in such cases but rather ensures a profit allocation that is (more) in line with economic realities.

3.3 The Transactional Net Margin Method (TNMM)

At last, we have arrived at the TNMM. By now, you are already familiar with the most important aspects of the TNMM, namely, that it is based on a comparison of net margins realized by a tested party which exhibits the functional profile of a routine entity. So, let's directly look at how the TNMM works in practice.[41]

The most important issue to grasp is highlighted by the OECD in Paragraph 2.64 OECD-GL:

[41]The guidance provided in this chapter applies 1:1 to the comparable profits method (CPM) with which the US readers will be more familiar (in fact, TNMM can be dubbed the "European cousin" of the CPM)—Thanks to prof. Eden for pointing out the need to clarify this issue more explicitly.

> [The TNMM] examines the net profit relative to an appropriate base (e.g. costs, sales, assets) that a taxpayer realises from a controlled transaction [. . .]. Thus, a transactional net margin method **operates in a manner similar to the cost plus and resale price methods**. [. . .] the net profit indicator of the taxpayer from the controlled transaction [. . .] should ideally be established by reference to the net profit indicator that the same taxpayer earns in comparable uncontrolled transactions, i.e. by reference to "internal comparables" [. . .]. Where this is not possible, the net margin that would have been earned in comparable transactions by an independent enterprise ("external comparables") may serve as a guide [. . .]. A **functional analysis** of the controlled and uncontrolled transactions is required to determine whether the transactions are comparable and what adjustments may be necessary to obtain reliable results.

In other words, the underlying rationale of the TNMM does not differ from the "traditional" methods; it is just much easier to apply. The reason for this is quite simple: While you will often have a hard time ascertaining an adequate degree of comparability for applying the RPM (see above) let alone identifying/obtaining the financial data required for conducting a comparability analysis, it will be feasible 100% of the time to identify external comparables that operate in a comparable industry and that are reasonably similar to a tested party exhibiting a routine functional profile. Also, importantly, for such routine comparables, financial data is readily available in the commercial databases.[42] Hence, while the OECD somewhat awkwardly states that an analysis of these external comparables "may serve as a guide," you will find that in practice easily more than 50% of the transfer pricing analysis are based on the TNMM (including variants of the cost-plus method that are applied on a full costs basis and thus almost indistinguishable from TNMM).

The one cardinal sin, which you must avoid, is to fall into the trap of applying the TNMM as a sort of default method without considering the specific facts and circumstances of the controlled transaction. When applying the TNMM, you first must absolutely make sure that (1) you have accurately delineated the transaction and (2) you have a rock-solid functional and risk analysis. A clear-cut red flag against applying the TNMM would be a tested party making unique and valuable contributions to the success of the business, i.e., economic ownership of substantial intangible assets. The great danger in such cases is that tax auditors may challenge that the routine classification of the tested party is false and that, because both transacting parties are making unique and valuable contributions, a "two-sided" method (this means the profit split method) ought to be applied as the more reliable method. Such challenges are the most dangerous challenges you can face, as the impact of respective transfer pricing adjustments will systematically translate into

[42] Naturally the notion of 100% availability is an exaggeration intended to emphasize a key point—please see Step 3a of the TNMM decision tree for a more realistic assessment. A substantial advantage of identifying routine comparables, especially comparables with a low turnover (i.e., below €20 Mio), is that their business activities tend to be rather simple, which means that functional comparability can be assessed in a rather straightforward manner and the financial data will require no (few) adjustments (i.e., working capital adjustments are unlikely to have substantial effects, and the reliability of the comparison is not limited by the lack of availability of segmented P&L data).

adjustments of the most extreme kind, i.e., allocating a part of the residual profit to an entity that previously was only allocated a comparatively small routine remuneration.[43] Hence, the more extensive the functional profile of the tested party, the more careful you must be in justifying that the TNMM is indeed the most reliable method; i.e., you would have to document that any intangible of the tested party is of "nonunique" nature (see OECD-GL 2017a, Paragraph 2.66).

Also, make no mistake; the adjustments mentioned by the OECD do not offer any shelter from these challenges. Adjustments, as understood in the context of the TNMM, should only compensate for comparatively minor differences such as differences in the working capital between tested party and external comparables (i.e., inventory levels of differences in accounts payable and accounts receivable—see Paragraph 3.49). Such adjustments, however, can never compensate for substantial differences in the functional profile. Many consulting firms will often automatically perform these adjustments when calculating the (inter-quartile) arm's length range—if applied without regard to the specific situation, however, these automatic adjustments do not reflect a sensible approach. As emphasized by the OECD (Paragraph 3.52): "It is not always the case that adjustments are warranted. For instance, an adjustment for differences in accounts receivable may not be particularly useful if major differences in accounting standards were also present that could not be resolved. Likewise, sophisticated adjustments are sometimes applied to create the false impression that the outcome of the comparables search is 'scientific', reliable and accurate." In other words, if only minor differences in working capital exist, you really do not need to bother making adjustment calculations, and if material adjustments are deemed to be required, they indicate that the degree of comparability might be considered to be insufficient to start with. To stay away from trouble, you should spend more time on the functional analysis (and manual screening of external comparables) rather than engaging in complex adjustment calculations that are prone to be challenged by the tax authorities.

Figure 3.13 summarizes the basics of the TNMM (the figure illustrates a tested party acting as a distributor—but the TNMM would also apply to routine entities rendering services, including contract manufacturing or contract research[44]):

The **TNMM decision tree** can be summarized as follows:

1. Have we excluded the applicability of traditional transfer pricing methods (CUP, RPM, C+[45])?

---

[43] Adjustments based on a re-classification and the respective discussions with the tax authorities will be the most confrontational discussions during an audit. Generally, you can compromise on each and every issue in transfer pricing, EXCEPT on the classification of the tested party. Often you can happily surrender 1–2% points when discussing the arm's length nature of target margins, while compromising on the classification of the entity will result in adjustments that will greatly exceed an adjusted target margin (especially when we are talking about IP centric business models).

[44] Note: Contract manufacturing and contract research are discussed below (see Sect. 3.5).

[45] Do not be confused by the inclusion of the C+ method here—the sub-section on the C+ will clarify the differences between C+ and TNMM.

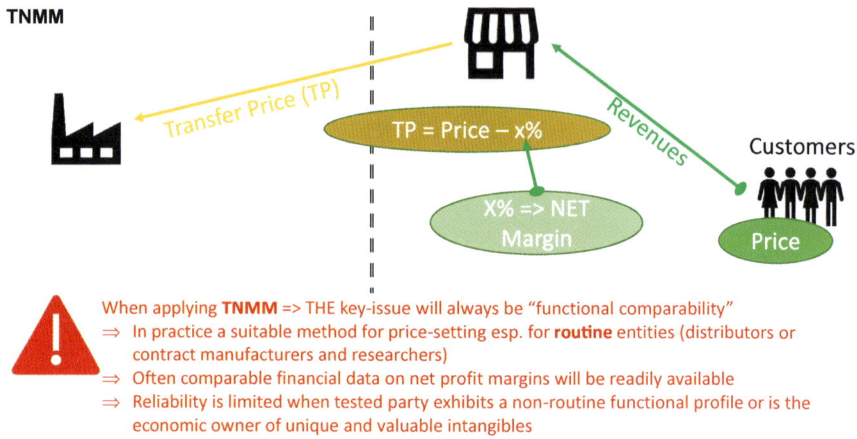

Fig. 3.13 Applying the TNMM (source: own Illustration)

(a) If "yes," good => but really, you can only reasonably hope to exclude the applicability of the CUP and should document your reasons just as before.
(b) If "no" or you were "unsure" => the rationale of the TNMM is not systematically different from RPM or C+. Hence, it will almost in all cases be feasible to utilize the TNMM "complementary" to the other methods, and you should devote respective care in explaining your selection of the transfer pricing method. Again, please do not utilize the TNMM as a default method.

2. Can we identify a tested party exhibiting a routine-type functional and risk profile?

(a) If "yes," we have established *the* most vital precondition for applying the TNMM (compare also the RPM decision tree above).
(b) If "no," you will likely have to discard the TNMM as the most appropriate transfer pricing methods. Depending on the specific case at hand, you may find yourself in a position where the TNMM can be chosen as a method of last resort—i.e., because you cannot identify suitable comparable data. In such a situation, you are well advised to proceed with caution; to mitigate risks, you may want to consider applying two methods as well as devoting additional efforts to document the arm's length considerations made by the parties (i.e., emphasizing the business rationale of the price-setting mechanism and referring to specific features of the relevant industry). In any case, you will have to pay special attention to delineating the relevant intangibles.

3. Can we identify sufficiently reliable data for the comparability analysis?

(a) If "yes," you will have to provide a detailed documentation on the search process. When applying the TNMM commercial databases will in most cases contain a sufficient number of comparable companies. In the last couple of years, benchmarking studies have increasingly "degenerated" into a "commodity." You should, however, avoid succumbing to complacency regarding the quality of benchmarks studies. There are severe differences in the quality of benchmark studies, and most tax authorities are versed enough to successfully attack benchmark studies when pushing for transfer pricing adjustments. Depending on your transfer pricing system, i.e., especially in case you have implemented a system build on target margins, you need to devote care to ensure that minimal quality standards are observed => a detailed "Checklist for Benchmark Studies" that guides you through a step-by-step process of adequately dealing with benchmark studies is provided in Annex B.[46]

(b) If "no" or "maybe," you will have to cope with the situation as best as possible. It can happen, that, despite your best efforts to follow Step 3a, the quality of the identified comparables seems a bit shaky. Don't panic, rather look back at Step 2a, and confirm that you are 100% sure of your functional analysis and that the TNMM is indeed the most appropriate method. Sometimes you simply cannot put yourself in a better position. This is, thankfully, also explicitly recognized by the OECD in OECD-GL (2017a), Paragraph 3.39: "[...] even when in cases where comparable data are scarce and imperfect, the selection of the most appropriate transfer pricing method should be consistent with the functional analysis of the parties." In other words, by diligently applying the methodological approach outlined above, you will effectively prevent the tax authorities from construing a challenge based on applying the profit split method and thus escape the systematically most dangerous challenges (see above)—and that is a positive to be sure.

Case Study: Utilizing the TNMM to Defend the Arm's Length Nature of Profit Allocations Within the Prima Group

As illustrated by the case study in the previous section, the comparability analysis based on the RPM (gross margins) merely enabled some tentative conclusions and arguments in support of the arm's length nature of the transfer prices agreed between Prima GmbH and its subsidiaries. External data for routine distributors of Electronic Consumer Products is readily available[47]; when performing a pan-European benchmark (which would be a sensible proposition for Prima), the first step would be to select an appropriate NACE-Code[48] (e.g., 4643 *wholesale of electrical household*

[46]Also, for applying a comparability analysis, the OECD provides a step-by-step approach that is considered accepted good practice (OECD-GL 2017a, Paragraph, 3.4). While following this process is not compulsory, it makes good sense to use it as a general orientation. Most of the steps reflect the lessons contained this book and thus provide a sensible summary of the lessons learned thus far—and to identify open issues which may have not been addressed in detail thus far. As we have already progressed through Step 1 to Step 6 at this point, the following case study (see below), in conjunction with the guidance provided in Annex C, constitutes an example of Step 7.

[47]For illustrative purposes, we utilize a publicly available generic benchmark study based on the Bureau van Dijk database; Source: Brem and Tucha (2013).

[48]To ensure a sufficiently large sample size, it is good practice not to be too restrictive when selecting appropriate NACE codes. Having conducted and reviewed scores of benchmark studies, it

NACE 4650		2008	2009	2010	Average
	Lower Quartile	1.23%	0.74%	0.85%	0.94%
Western Europe	*Median*	*3.42%*	*2.91%*	*2.83%*	3.05%
	Upper Quartile	7.19%	6.15%	6.01%	6.45%
	Lower Quartile	0.75%	0.59%	0.76%	0.70%
Eastern Europe	*Median*	*2.59%*	*2.45%*	*3.15%*	2.73%
	Upper Quartile	7.46%	5.96%	7.42%	6.95%

Fig. 3.14 Arm's length ranges for Prima distributors (Source: own illustration (based on Brem and Tucha 2013))

appliance or 4650 *wholesale of electronic and communication equipment*) as well as the relevant (appropriate) economic region. Figure 3.14 summarizes an exemplary result for the NACE code 4650 in Western as well as in Eastern Europe for the period 2008–2010.

Some quick remarks regarding the interquartile range illustrated above (for general comments on benchmarking, see Annex B):

- The interquartile range is rather wide => this is (likely) attributable to the fact that this is a "generic benchmark," i.e., a manual (qualitative) screening for identifying individual comparables was not conducted. A wide range signals a "heterogeneous" composition of the comparable companies, which in turn may (!) indicate a rather low degree of comparability => as a result, you should be cautious and refrain from setting target margins too close to either upper or lower quartile.
- There are hardly any material inter-regional differences => considering that the anticipated result for routine entities, i.e., small but stable profits, applies on a global scale, this is hardly surprising. While this rationale should generally also be confirmed when restricting the search to a single country, the results for local (national) comparables may differ somewhat on account of an extremely small sample. When defending your margins in countries such as Italy or in some of the BRICS countries (China, India), you should, however, be aware that the local authorities will insist on utilizing local comparables.[49] Whether or not to walk

seems evident that the allocation of companies to a specific NACE Code is not always 100% clear-cut. Being a little more tolerant on the NACE code has no downside—in some cases, it will translate into a higher workload for the manual screening, but it will generally enhance the quality of your analysis (the trade-off will generally be positive).

[49] In most cases, the economic rationale of insisting on local comparables is extremely weak. When applying TNMM, we are focused on determining an appropriate remuneration for a routine activity rather than allocating the residual profit. From a policy perspective, this implies that "tinkering" with margins does not provide MNEs with an enticing lever for tax avoidance (i.e., target margins and target ranges will mostly be calibrated based on business considerations—see below—rather than tax optimization. From an economic perspective, it would thus seem sensible to allow the taxpayers a reasonable leeway regarding his analytical approach toward benchmarking. The OECD

through the motions of preparing a benchmark based on local comparables will depend on the trade-offs in each individual case.
- The identified interquartile range is rather stable over time. Such results are common in day-to-day practice and are, again, commensurate with the anticipated results for routine entities
- The **key takeaway**: Once you have identified that the TNMM is the most appropriate method, you have successfully eliminated the "systemic risk" of your transfer pricing system. To be sure, there might still be (heated) discussions about the arm's length nature of a specific margin, but that risk will be manageable ("known" and "quantifiable").

Taken with a grain of salt (see above comments), the identified inter-quartile range provides an appropriate basis on which to proceed with our analysis. Please note the following: (1) The analysis is not "finished" once you have determined an interquartile range, as you will always have to "interpret" the data (see Step 8 and Step 9 of OECD-GL, Paragraph 3.4—see also Chap. 2); (2) We could spend a lot of time debating the "appropriateness" of the interquartile range (but we won't)[50]; (3) most importantly, we should think about how best to "operationalize" the inter-quartile range for the Prima Group (i.e., being mindful of trade-offs between tax and management objectives).

In respect to issue (3), it is always sensible to determine whether (how) the identified interquartile range can be adopted as a "target range." A target range is a pragmatic tool to verify whether the net margin realized by a tested party (in our case, the local Prima subsidiaries performing routine distribution services) reflects an arm's length "remuneration"[51] (ex post). In case the net margin falls into the target

---

should weigh-in much more heavily in the discourse by clearly stating that pan-regional benchmarks should be accepted unless extraordinary economic circumstances prevail that render a pan-regional analysis unreliable. In such cases, the burden of proof should be resting with the tax authorities on a case-by-case basis. To some extent, this might be wishful thinking, but such a regulation would be an obvious gain for everyone, except those harboring biased views of endemic tax avoidance practices.

[50]Well, we should at least briefly elaborate on arm's length ranges a bit in this footnote. In day-to-day transfer pricing, inter-quartile ranges are quite often the subject of debate between MNEs and tax authorities, as an adjustment by 1 or 2% may translate in a multi-million transfer pricing adjustment (if you are dealing with big MNEs—but even in smaller cases, the adjustments are unpleasant). Conceptionally, every margin within the inter-quartile range reflects arm's length conditions. When considering that utilizing the inter-quartile range implies discarding 50% of the identified comparables as (statistical) "outliers," one could argue that relying on the inter-quartile range already reflects a rather conservative approach. At least, tax authorities should concede that inter-quartile ranges are not a suitable mechanism (lever) for engaging in tax avoidance. Still, as a rule, tax authorities are prone to gravitate toward the median (China even explicitly disqualified any margin below the median for determining an arm's length remuneration for local (Chinese) routine entities (see SAT Public Notice [2017] No.6, Article 25). Hence, you should be mindful of respective aggressive behavior by the tax authorities when setting your target range (see below) and aim to "stay away from the fringes."

[51]Remuneration is used quite deliberately in this context, as it appropriately reflects the routine nature of the functions performed by the Prima Subsidiaries. Considering that the distribution

range, it is concluded that the prices (in our case, commission rate or resale margin) that were agreed between the Prima GmbH and the subsidiaries (ex ante) were commensurate with the arm's length standard. Utilizing a target range thus allows to operationalize the comparability analysis (TNMM) in a way that it triggers a sort of "feedback loop." This feedback loop constitutes (arguably) the best way to reconcile the "price-setting approach" (ex ante) with the "outcome-testing approach" (ex post). These approaches have often been interpreted as reflecting a fundamentally opposed interpretation of the arm's length principles. In a nutshell, the outcome-testing approach stipulates that taxpayers should test the actual outcome of their controlled transactions to demonstrate that the conditions of these transactions were consistent with the arm's length principle, whereas the price-setting approach requires taxpayers to establish transfer pricing documentation that demonstrates that they have made reasonable efforts to comply with the arm's length principle at the time their intra-group transactions were undertaken based on information that was reasonably available to them at that moment. These quite different theoretical approaches are of high relevance in day-to-day practice, as most tax authorities do have a clear preference for one of these approaches (and tend to challenge the other approach).[52] A tax authority following the outcome testing approach would challenge the arm's length transfer prices in case the net margins fall outside of the identified arm's length range and demand a "compensating adjustment" to push (or pull) the net margin to fall within the arm's length range. A tax authority adhering to the price-setting approach, however, would often deny a respective compensating adjustment, based on the notion that independent third parties would not agree to such a retroactive payment. Which of the two approaches is to be considered "superior" is ultimately a moot point. It could be argued that on a stand-alone basis, neither of the two is 100% convincing insofar as third parties obviously conduct ex ante as well as ex post negotiations. While a price will always be negotiated ex ante, it frequently occurs in the context of services that the respective fees are often (fiercely) negotiated in the final stages of the projects (i.e., when the agreed milestones or deliverables are not sufficiently clear and when additional work is required).[53] The compromise outlined by the EUJTPF (see EUJTPF, Sec. 4.2) nicely established sensible middle-ground that should be

---

activities are not performed autonomously, they reflect, from an economic perspective, the provision of services rather than a sales activity.

[52]The German tax authorities, for example, tend to put strong emphasis on the price-setting approach, while the IRS seems much more comfortable with following the outcome-testing approach. It is somewhat difficult to rationalize these differences, and the historic origins do not seem worthwhile to explore at this point. For details on this issue, please refer to European Joint Transfer pricing Forum ("EUJTPF") (2013).

[53]Considering that intercompany transactions are akin to transaction between third parties having established long-term business relationships (i.e., think of key suppliers), both parties will certainly be willing to find a mutually agreeable solution in case unforeseen market developments have an impact on the originally agreed (budgeted) fee (again, referring to remuneration/fee for services rendered allows for a more sensible assessment of the arm's length nature of ex post adjustments from an economic perspective).

embraced by MNEs to comply with price-setting as well as with the outcome testing approach—pursuant to the pragmatic solution compensating adjustments shall be acceptable when the following conditions are met:

- "Before the relevant transaction or series of transactions, the taxpayer made reasonable efforts to achieve an arm's length outcome. This would normally be described in the transfer pricing documentation of the taxpayer" => The considerations outlined in Sect. 2.2 would be enough for ensuring compliance with this provision for Prima. In respect to the adjustment mechanism, the target margin should be defined ex ante. Also, it is highly recommended to clearly stipulate the adjustment calculations to be performed. It should also be clarified that a review of the price-setting would be compulsory in case the target range is missed repeatedly.[54]
- "The taxpayer makes the adjustment symmetrically in the accounts in both MS involved" => This condition is painfully obvious and should be considered a "given."
- "The taxpayer applies the same approach consistently over time" => This provision is not quite as obvious and should not be underestimated in practice. Taxpayers need to understand the fact that utilizing a target range implies the introduction of an "automatism." Committing to an automatism will limit the scope for any discretionary decisions by the management which will often be an obstacle to implementing a respective mechanism.[55]
- "The taxpayer makes the adjustment before filing the tax return" => Again, a rather obvious provision.
- "The taxpayer is able to explain for what reasons his forecast did not match the result achieved, when it is required by internal legislation in at least one of the MS involved."[56]

---

[54]Also, it should be made clear to the management team that the budgets and forecast must accurately reflect the agreed target range. Should a specific subsidiary suffer permanent losses (see Prima Spain) which will continue based on the current budgets, an adjustment of the agreed prices (commission rates) must be triggered as the losses indicate that the local entity cannot realize an arm's length profit based on the prevailing market conditions.

[55]While the automatic nature of the adjustment limits the scope for discretionary decisions, the contractual provisions for the adjustment mechanism can (should) contain appropriate solutions for extraordinary situations (i.e., a "grace period" for market-entry phases or an "escape clause" in case of (severe) losses on group level). The responsible managers should actively participate in developing the adjustment mechanism to ensure ownership and efficient implementation.

[56]Naturally, this will translate into an additional administrative burden. This burden should not be overestimated, however, as conducting a respective analysis will be sensible irrespective of tax considerations (i.e., in the case of Prima Spain, it would have to be evaluated whether continuing to be active on the Spanish market with a subsidiary is sensible—evaluating whether switching to an independent sales agent may be beneficial would certainly be worthwhile from a management perspective).

Taking the above into account, a sensible target range and adjustment mechanism for Prima could be defined as follows (this could be stipulated in an annex to the respective intercompany agreement)[57]:

- *Target Range*: Lower Bound => 1.5%// Upper Bound => 4.5%
  - The Target Range was determined by adding/subtracting 1.5% from the median (approx. 3% see above). Naturally, different approaches would be feasible. You should aim at minimizing the need for adjustments by stipulating a sufficiently wide target range—observing the inter-quartile range as sort of natural boundary (in the case at hand, it would also seem sensible for Prima to stipulate an upper bound of about 6% which could be rationalized "moving" 1% toward the median from both lower and upper quartile).
- *Adjustment Mechanism*: In case that the EBIT margin realized by the Distributor falls outside of the Target Range, it is agreed by the Parties that the result reflects a market situation that has been substantially altered and that the reasons for the deviating margins are beyond the control of the Distributor—requiring an automatic transfer pricing adjustment. In case of adjustments, Prima GmbH, acting as the entrepreneur, is (1) entitled to any profits exceeding the upper end of the target range as well as (2) liable for all losses exceeding lower end of the target range. Consequently, the Parties agree that adjustment payments will have to be performed in order to ensure that the EBIT margin of the Distributor equals either the lower end (in case of "extreme" losses) or the upper end (in case of "extreme" profits) of the target range (caution: beware of implications with customs[58]):

[57]This exemplary mechanism reflects a "plain vanilla" type of solution. You can certainly get more creative. Often you will have to be more creative to avoid an overly burdensome adjustment mechanism, i.e., avoiding a situation in which compensating adjustments become the norm rather than the exception. Most of us will have experienced how difficult it is to hit a targeted margin (narrow range) especially when dealing with a pricing system based on commissions. Hence, you will have to find ways to increase the width of the Target Range and increase the flexibility of the adjustment mechanism. One alternative is to define a "tolerance range" that encompasses the target range and to stipulate that within a single financial year, the margins can fluctuate within the tolerance range and that an adjustment will only be triggered in case the 3-year average falls outside the target range. Depending on the specific business model such an alternative can make sense—and can be justified (naturally, the risks of having to tangle with the tax authorities will increase proportionately to your level of creativity—so, best keep it within reasonable limits). The Grace period and Safeguard Clause stipulated below are a "soft" mechanism for the management to exercise at least a limited amount of discretion—such clauses can be vital to ensure management ownership when implementing an adjustment mechanism.

[58]A word of caution must be made in respect to the implementation of adjustments: While the suggested adjustment procedure is rather straightforward from a transfer pricing perspective and is thus presented as a "positive" or "beneficial" mechanism in the case for Prima, you should be careful when it comes to retroactively adjusting your customs declarations. In my experience, it is not all fun to deal with customs issues, as the regulations (and valuation approaches) appear to be rather inflexible. Unfortunately, the OECD has adopted a somewhat aloof position on this issue and states that: "*Cooperation between income tax and customs administrations within a country in evaluating transfer prices is becoming more common and this should help to reduce the number of*

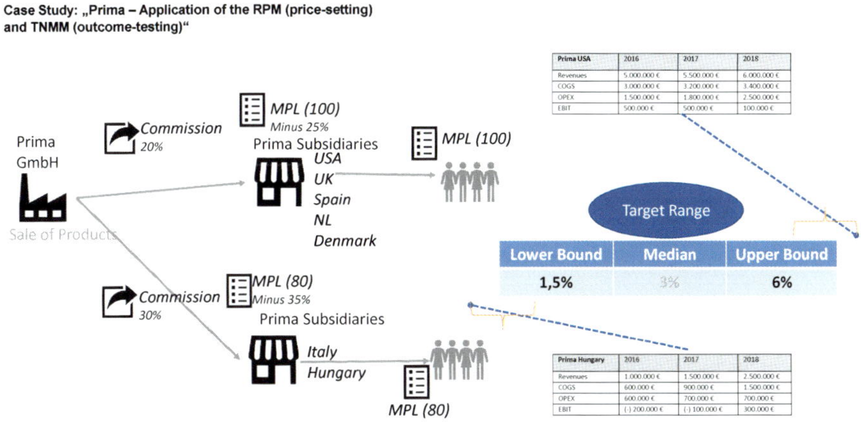

Fig. 3.15 Refined price-setting mechanism for the Prima Group (source: own Illustration)

– "Grace period": no automatic adjustments will be applicable until the respective Distributor has successfully completed the market-entry (i.e., not prior to completing the third year of local operations).
– "Safeguard clause": In case the adjustment mechanism stipulated above fails to result in economically sensible situations, i.e., if idiosyncratic and unforeseeable developments impact the financial results of the Distributor, the Parties will contemporaneously negotiate a mutually acceptable solution which appropriately reflects the spirit of these guidelines and ensures an arm's length outcome. Respective exemptions from the adjustment mechanism are to be appropriately documented.

Figure 3.15 builds on the case study shown in the RPM section. In addition to the applied discounts from the MPL and commission rates, it illustrates the abbreviated P&Ls of the subsidiaries in the USA and Hungary[59] as well as the target range discussed above.

As illustrated in Fig. 3.15, the Prima subsidiary located in Hungary realized margins below the target range in 2016 and 2017, while realizing a net margin of 12% in 2018 (exceeding the upper bound). On aggregate, the Hungarian subsidiary realized a net margin of 0% during the 2016–2018 period. Considering that the Hungarian subsidiary progressed through a market-entry phase during the period

cases where customs valuations are found unacceptable for tax purposes or vice versa" (see OECD-GL, Paragraph 1.138). In real life that is just not happening—when having to deal with customs issues as a transfer pricing practitioner, I recommend starting by reading-up on the "Hamamatsu Case." The key-advice in respect to designing your adjustment mechanism is to ensure enough flexibility (suggestions are outlined below) and minimize the need for adjustments—i.e., adopt a "get it right the first time" approach.

[59] We will focus on discussing the USA and Hungary, as the respective arguments are immediately relevant for the other subsidiaries as well.

under review, the results merit some additional interpretation. As highlighted in the previous section, the fact that the Hungarian subsidiary suffered losses in 2016 and 2017 does not indicate non-arm's length pricing. It is rather evident that the more favorable terms extended to the Hungarian subsidiary (i.e., a higher commission rate compared to that agreed between Prima GmbH and other subsidiaries and the independent agent in Australia) shielded the local agent from even higher losses. Considering that the calibration of the commission enabled the local entity to break-even after operating for 3 years (which is often considered by tax authorities to constitute default duration for market-entry[60]), the implied support for the market-entry appears adequate. Assuming that the entity has attained a "steady state" by 2019, it is recommended that whether the prevailing economic conditions still justify, the higher commission rates should be assessed—note that the net margin for 2018 exceeds the upper bound of the target range (again, be mindful to avoid comparing "apples" and "oranges," i.e., differentiate between commission and resale business—see Sect. 2.2[61]).

For the Prima subsidiary located in the USA, the (unadjusted) net margins realized in 2016 and 2017 would trigger the application of the adjustment mechanism.[62] Due to the materially lower margin realized in 2018, however, the profitability of the US subsidiary falls within the target range when considering the 3-year average. Considering that even in 2016 and 2017 the (unadjusted) margins only slightly exceeded the upper bound of the target range, it could be deduced that allowing a reasonable degree of flexibility seems sensible. A situation in which you would perform separate downward adjustments (i.e., issuing debit notes to the US subsidiary) in 2016 and 2017 and an upward adjustment (i.e., issuing a credit note) in 2018 only to attain a similar net result to a situation without performing any adjustments appears hardly desirable. Paradoxically, however, the separate adjustments are likely to translate into a more viable tax position.[63] Ultimately, there is no

[60]Naturally, there is no empiric justification for limiting a market-entry phase to 3 years, as the duration may substantially vary depending on the specific facts and circumstances of each individual case. It is, however, highly recommended to elaborate (document) on these circumstances in case you want to apply a longer market-entry phase.

[61]As highlighted above, the fact that the commission revenues hit the P&L of the Hungarian entity without corresponding COGS will have an impact on the margin. For the Hungarian subsidiary, however, only about 22% of the revenues relate to the commission business. Adjusting the net margin of the Hungarian subsidiary to the retail business yields a margin of 10.2% (instead of the 12% unadjusted mentioned above). While the conclusion, namely, that reviewing the arm's length nature of the pricing due to exceeding the upper bound of the target range, thus remains valid, this example should illustrate the need for performing appropriate adjustments (i.e., an appropriate level of segmentation).

[62]The adjusted margins of the US subsidiary would fall within the arm's length range.

[63]One critical issue in this regard is to be seen in the fact that many tax and transfer pricing regulations are focused on assessing the arm's length principle in view of a single financial year. Hence, while there is ample scope for designing a sensible adjustment mechanism from an economic perspective (see also footnote above), the tax viability of a specific mechanism should be reviewed by a local tax advisor to ensure compliance with formal requirements.

"one-size-fits-all" solution, and you will always have to deal with the trade-off between tax viability and administrative burden. Provided that the fluctuations remain within reasonable limits (i.e., commensurate with the functional profile of the tested party), there is generally no reason, from an economic perspective, to dispute the arm's length nature of the transfer prices agreed between the parties. The only thing you cannot afford is to be complacent.

The **bottom line** for the TNMM section is simple: You need to actively monitor the net margins of the routine entities within your group if you want to minimize transfer pricing-related tax risks.[64]

Box 3.3 Restating the Lesson
Arm's Length Net Margins Should Make Everyone Happy

It may be counterintuitive, but when viewed from a perspective that is focused on minimizing systemic risks, the TNMM is not about net margins or benchmarking. It is really about conducting a solid functional and risk analysis and subsequently deriving a clandestine classification of the tested party as a "routine entity." Having established a respective classification, you have essentially removed the residual profits (losses) from the discussions with tax authorities. Once it is agreed that the tested party does not make unique and valuable contributions, it should automatically be agreed that a remuneration that ensures small but stable profits will reflect arm's length conditions.

Identifying a range of arm's length profit margins for a specific business activity within a specific industry (within a specific geographic area) is ultimately a "technicality." As the net margins, compared to prices or gross margins, are much less sensitive to differences in individual comparability factors, it will always be feasible to at least find a reliable approximation of an arm's length net margin for a tested party. While there will always remain discussions about the arm's length range, especially if the range applied by a specific MNE is excessively broad, we can rather be confident that the discussions we are dealing within this context cannot be labeled as aggressive tax planning.

Some of the developing countries (notably China and India) are adopting the position that TNMM-based remunerations for the local subsidiaries of global MNEs are putting them at a systemic disadvantage. They reason that the synergies realized from "location specific advantages" (i.e., access to the local

(continued)

[64]One additional word of caution—I have been growing-up consulting in the SME segment, where pragmatic approaches as outlined above are likely to be a best fit. Recently, I have had the pleasure to work for a rather sizeable MNE and the one key takeaway for me was that if the stakes are raised (i.e. if you are looking at a cumulative transaction volume of 800 Mio. € in a 5-year period for a single subsidiary (sale of goods, applying modified RPM) then each % point matters plenty. It should not even be a choice—you either proactively manage your margins and adjust your pricing, or you will face painful adjustments.

Box 3.3 (continued)
market and lower labor costs) should at least partially be shared by higher profit margins (higher markups on costs). There certainly is a good argument for recognizing location-specific advantages ("LSAs") in the context of the comparability analysis, especially when using pan-regional approaches to benchmarking—when you succeed in identifying sufficiently reliable local comparables, however, there seems to be no reason for any additional adjustments of the resulting arm's length range, as the profitability of the local comparables would reflect the impact of LSAs. The OECD has correctly pointed out that LSAs do not constitute intangibles that would be attributable to the local entities. Consequently, the application of the TNMM, when it qualifies as the most appropriate method, will ensure an appropriate (arm's length) allocation of profits.

As highlighted above, there is no economic reason why a routine entity that performs low-value-added functions should be allocated a share in the residual profits of an MNE. This rationale applies irrespective of the size of the operations; i.e., routine entities might be large-scale operations; mere scale doesn't magically transform the quality of the value-added contributions. From a policy perspective, there seems to be good cause to adopt a somewhat more relaxed approach to TNMM-based transfer pricing systems => it is *the* "low-risk" situation and certainly not the root cause for base erosion and profit shifting.

3.4 The Profit Split Method (PSM)

Your attitude regarding the PSM says a lot about your character as transfer pricing consultant. It would not be entirely inaccurate to claim that the PSM is a method for the brave. Some people will certainly believe this—although such a flamboyant claim is not touching the heart of the nature of the PSM. It is, however, a frequent observation that practitioners who on principle are shying away from the PSM are not worth their salt. Considering that we only have five transfer pricing methods at our disposal, it is just poor strategy to discard one method—most often just because one does not feel entirely "comfortable" with the degree of (perceived) uncertainty involved in building a transfer pricing system based on the PSM. It is akin to playing chess without ever truly utilizing the Knight, just because you do not fancy the way it moves across the board. Ultimately, you will not win against decent opposition. So, please, in your own interest, take the PSM seriously and do not skip to the next chapter in search of the (beloved) Cost-Plus Method (Fig. 3.16).

When discussing the RPM as well as the TNMM, we put a lot of emphasis on identifying the tested party. Clear and unambiguous identification of a tested party will make your life easier, as you will automatically establish an expectation of the ultimate profit allocation; i.e., the tested party should realize a profit margin within a

OECD Guidelines 2017, Paragraph 2.114

The transactional profit split method **first identifies the profits to be split** for the associated enterprises from the controlled transactions in which the associated enterprises are engaged (the "combined profits"). References to "profits" should be taken as applying equally to losses. [...]. It **then splits those combined profits** between the associated enterprises on an economically valid basis that **approximates the division of profits that would have been anticipated and reflected in an agreement made at arm's length.**

Fig. 3.16 Profit split method (source: OECD)

range of profits observed for comparable companies, while the residual profit (loss) will be allocated to the entrepreneur (non-tested party). The subsequent application of a one-sided method as well as the corresponding comparability analysis will require some effort and analytical acumen, but they are not exactly rocket science either. As stressed above, you are predominantly talking about technicalities while the systemic risks are eliminated (mitigated) by a thorough functional and risk analysis and the resulting choice of the tested party.

Considering this background, the PSM is best understood as the ultimate safeguard against systemic risk; i.e., in all cases where you are not able to identify a clear and unambiguous tested party, you should at least consider whether the PSM constitutes a feasible alternative.

There is no denying it, a two-sided analysis will (ostensibly) require more effort than a one-sided analysis. But, considering that uncertainty in respect to the identification of the tested party translates to systemic risk, i.e., the allocation of the residual profit is likely to be contested by the tax authorities, the trade-off of performing a two-sided analysis will almost always be positive. The following would be considered sensible "red flags" (typical situations) triggering the use of the PSM[65]:

- You are looking at a "highly integrated" value chain; **i.e.**, multiple parties make important contributions to key value-added functions, which cannot appropriately (easily) be segmented.[66]

[65]The EU, specifically the EUJTPF, is currently (i.e., in the beginning of 2019) in the process of compiling guidance (EUJTPF 2018). The working paper constitutes a sensible summary of the issue at hand but fails to make a positive contribution (i.e., it does not add much to the insights or discussions on OECD level) (EUJTPF 2019). In this context, the EU essentially confirmed the interpretation reflected in this OECD-GL. The strong-point of the report is the detailed discussion of possible profit-splitting factors to be applied.

[66]In the context of the public discussion of the OECD BEPS project on the PSM, there was some intense debate directed at whether the nature of the integration triggering application of the PSM should be "sequential" or "parallel." While the argument that the advantages of the PSM may be more pronounced when dealing with parallel integration are sensible (as sequential integration will generally permit some degree of delineation or segmentation), this discussion is (arguably) not decisive for practical purposes. So, if the level of integration is high, look closely at the PSM as the potentially most appropriate method and do not get sidetracked by philosophical musings about parallel and sequential integration.

- Multiple parties contribute (unique and valuable[67]) intangibles. Yes, there is an overlap with the first bullet, but the contribution of unique and valuable intangibles is *the* most important qualitative "red flag" triggering a profit split. In this context, a respective party would not have to contribute a lot (any) of additional functions, as the mere contribution of one unique and valuable intangible will disqualify such a party from being classified as tested party.
- The business model is focused on exploiting IP (with one entity permitting a related party to use a brand or technological know-how); i.e., we are talking license or franchise agreements. In practice, you will often see that CUPs are applied for validating the arm's length nature of the respective royalties and fees. As we have learned above, however, the comparability for an appropriate application of a CUP is rather prohibitive. While you will find data in commercial license databases, you should not place too much trust in the (stand-alone) results.[68] In such cases, it is recommended that a secondary analysis based on the PSM be conducted.
- The business relationship to customers is not focused on individual products or services, but rather characterized by providing a bundle of products and services in the context of projects to which multiple parties make contributions. While there are project-based businesses which allow for the application of one-sided methods, there is a high likelihood that, especially for complex projects, the reliability of a one-sided method is limited.

The common element of the trigger points listed above is that a one-sided analysis will systematically result in a "skewed" and one-sided profit allocation.[69] Applying the PSM will result in a more "balanced" profit allocation and thus mitigate

[67]Adding "unique" and "valuable" here may be counterintuitive for some, as it could be argued that most intangibles can be considered unique and valuable. In a transfer pricing context, however, this distinction or qualification is quite important—it is also tricky and somewhat arbitrary. Ultimately, the point here is that not all intangibles will justify an allocation of the residual profit to the respective economic owner. The OCED provides the following example (OECD-GL, Paragraph 6.10): "For example, consider a situation in which an enterprise performs a service using non-unique know-how, where other comparable service providers have comparable know-how. In that case, even though know-how constitutes an intangible, it may be determined under the facts and circumstances that the know-how does not justify allocating a premium return to the enterprise, over and above normal returns earned by comparable independent providers of similar services that use comparable non-unique know-how." The relevant definitions are provided in Paragraph 6.17 as well as section D.1.3. of Chapter 1; unfortunately, these definitions are not 100% conclusive. Hence, you will have to make a subjective judgment that considers the facts of the case at hand as best as possible—there will often be no single best solution, but by proactively addressing the issue, you at least mitigate the risk of walking into an unidentified risk.

[68]This will be illustrated in the case study variation presented in Annex C.

[69]Now, obviously, the CUP is not a one-sided method as such, but the mechanics and "risk profile" apply largely analogous to those of one-sided methods in this context. It should also be considered that the issue of intangibles received a lot of attention in the course of the BEPS project. The resulting modification of the OECD-GL essentially reflects a "debasement" of the CUP when applied in a situation such as identified above. The reason is straightforward; it is incredibly difficult (literally impossible) to fulfill the strict comparability requirements of a CUP when you conduct a

respective risks. While the respective explanation provided by the OECD is certainly correct, it arguably lacks the appropriate emphasis: "A further [i.e. one of the most important!] strength of the transactional profit split method is that it is less likely that either party to the controlled transaction will be left with an extreme and improbable profit result, since both parties to the transaction are evaluated. This aspect can be particularly important when analyzing the contributions by the parties in respect of the intangible property employed in the controlled transactions" (OECD-GL 2.119). In other words, in case you are in doubt as to whether your identification of the tested party is viable, the PSM is an ideal and efficient option for hedging your bet.

There is an additional sub-method of the PSM in our Toolbox that can be utilized for mitigating risks relating to the identified trigger points, the so-called residual profit split method (RPSM). The RPSM is essentially a PSM with an additional, preliminary, step. In this preliminary step, you will try to identify sub-processes or functions that can appropriately be "isolated" form the rest of the value chain. This can be tricky in the context of highly integrated value chains,[70] but you will encounter business models which are comprised of "IP heavy" high-value-added activities and low-value-added activities such as contract manufacturing. When applying the RPSM, you will first evaluate the low-value-added activities on a stand-alone basis and allocate an arm's length routine remuneration to the transaction party performing the respective function (i.e., by applying the TNMM). The immediate effect should be evident; you reduce the remaining, residual, profit to be allocated between the transacting parties. The (appealing) idea and effect of the RPSM is thus to remove a portion of the profits (the routine portion) from potential conflicts with tax authorities—as the working assumption is that a TNMM remuneration will be less susceptible to challenges than the PSM. When the relevant facts and circumstances of your case justify the application of the RPSM, you should consider taking advantage. There may, however, also be case in which the RPSM cannot be reliably applied or in which there are no (or only minimal) advantages compared to applying the PSM in one step.

Figures 3.17 and 3.18 illustrate the mechanism:

Before we proceed to the case study and the PSM, I want to embark on a brief detour to make sure that the importance of intangibles is properly understood from an economic perspective. It is vital to recognize that the special provisions for intangibles sketched above are not rooted in the purpose of facilitating tax or transfer pricing shenanigans but are rather accurate reflections of the impact intangibles have in value creation.

---

comprehensive analysis of the idiosyncratic features and functions (i.e., "DEMPE functions"—see below for details) that characterize a specific business model.

[70]You will not only have to identify a case in which it is sensible from a business or economic point of view to isolate these activities—but you will also require access to appropriately (reliably) segmented financial data (which will not always be available).

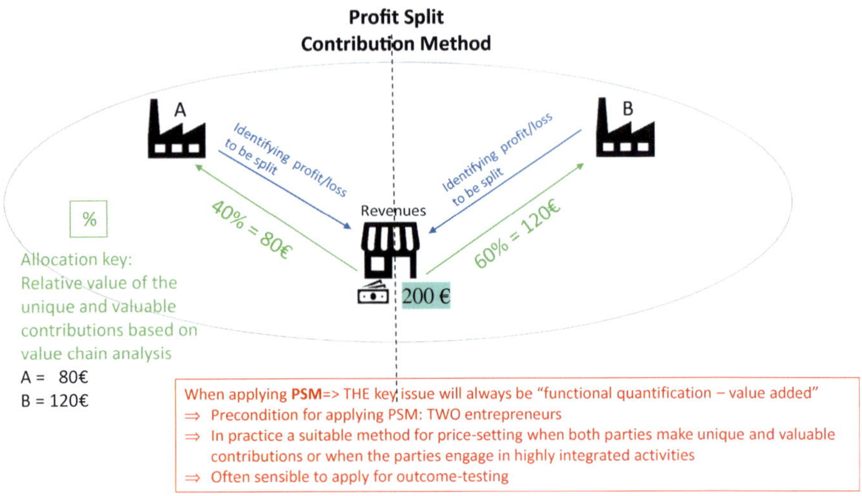

Fig. 3.17 Applying the profit split method—contribution method (source: own illustration)

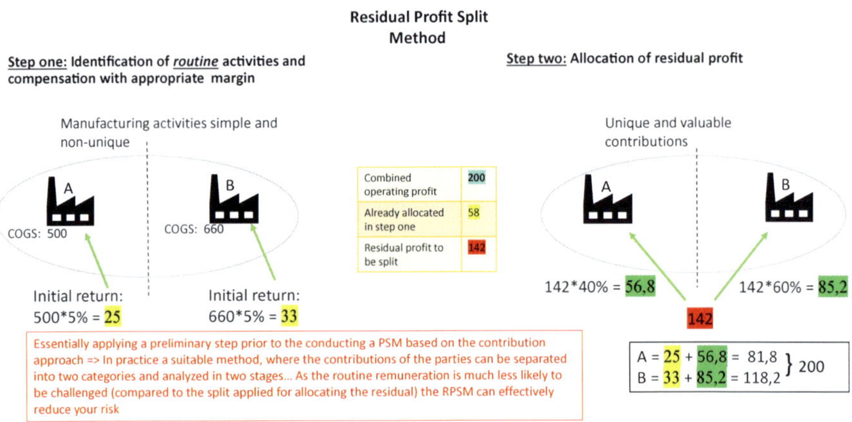

Fig. 3.18 Applying the residual profit method (source: own illustration)

Let us start with a drastic example, namely, the value of the "Burberry" brand.[71] Most of us will be surprised to learn that in 2017 Burberry destroyed unsold clothes and accessories and perfume worth £28.6m and that the total value of goods it has destroyed over the past 5 years was more than £90m. When you consider, however, that expensive fashion products such as Burberry are so-called Veblen Goods, i.e., goods for which the demand curve increases when the price is higher, the destruction of unsold clothes absolutely makes sense. In such a situation, the owner of the brand would perceive the destruction of unsold goods as an investment in protecting its

[71]This example is inspired by a blogpost of Worstall (2018).

brand (while selling at discounts would cannibalize the brand value). Of course, you do not build a brand by destroying goods. Rather you will have to invest heavily in advertising and marketing. Aside from the actual design (creative input of the designer), these functions contribute the core value-added in the fashion industry. Production does not matter. Neither does logistics.[72] From a transfer pricing perspective, it logically follows that the residual profits will be allocated to those entities contributing the unique and valuable intangibles and making the crucial strategic decision (entrepreneurs), while entities performing supporting functions will be allocated a small and stable (routine) remuneration. Now, in real life entrepreneurs frequently must stomach losses as well. So, while claiming residual profits is nice, an entrepreneur such as Burberry must ultimately also bear the costs of destroying the unsold products and faces the risk of an eroding brand value.[73] In fashion, your brand matters. It also matters how creative and "en vogue" your designer is. The most important intangibles and related functions can be contributed by comparatively few key-people. It is not unheard of that on a "headcount basis" these key-people may only account for a fraction of the total MNE headcount.

To evaluate whether the profit allocation reflects arm's length conditions (i.e., is in a sensible proportion to the value-added contributions), you must understand the idiosyncratic business model. What is important is that you look closely at the functions that are being performed, i.e., at the economic basis of the business not at the legal (ownership) structure. In this context, it is one of the most significant (and arguably "positive") contributions of the OECD BEPS project, that it was clarified that the mere legal ownership of an intangible does not entitle a specific entity to claim the residual profits attributable to the intangible. While the importance of legal ownership is relegated to merely a starting point for the analysis, the OECD introduced the so-called "DEMPE" concept and clarified that: "[…] *the ultimate allocation of the returns derived by the MNE group from the exploitation of intangibles, and the ultimate allocation of costs and other burdens related to intangibles among members of the MNE group, is accomplished by compensating members of the MNE group for functions performed, assets used, and risks assumed in the development, enhancement, maintenance, protection and exploitation of intangibles*" (OECD-GL, Paragraph 6.32). It is admittedly inevitable, for any qualitative analysis, that you will have to rely on subjective valuations. The DEMPE concept, however, enables tax authorities to effective question the economic

[72] Even the sales function (at the point of sale) will not be decisive for the success of most business models in the fashion industry; i.e., think about who is actual performing the functions at the cash register. Right, students, and interns who are happy to receive an appropriate remuneration—why should the organizational unit in which these students and the brick and mortar (or online) shops are aggregated be entitled to a share of the residual profit? Because they provide access to the local market? Seriously?

[73] So, if the goods-to-be-destroyed would have been in a warehouse operated by a routine sales entity in another jurisdiction, the economic owner of the brand making the strategic decision to destroy the products would also be responsible for the economic effects of that decision and bear the costs.

rationale of transfer pricing arrangements for intangibles and look beyond mere legal ownership.

When it can be substantiated that a few key-people perform the bulk of DEMPE functions,[74] it would undoubtedly reflect arm's length behavior to allocate the residual profits to the legal entity(ies) to whom these key-people are assigned (even if these happen to be located in a "low tax jurisdiction"). Yet, for some stakeholders, a "skewed" profit allocation that, based on qualitative assessments, is commensurate with the arm's length principle is perceived as "unfair." NGOs claiming to fight for a notion of "fair taxation" (such as the Tax Justice Network), for example, feel that "skewed" profit allocations are inherently abusive. A case in point is the campaign (by the Greens-European Foreign Alliance Group) against the fashion brand "Zara" (or its legal owner the MNE Inditex located in Spain). The claim that Zara engaged in large scale tax avoidance by abusive transfer pricing (allegedly syphoning profits to Ireland, the Netherlands, and Switzerland) was beautifully debunked by Maya Forstater by illustrating that only 3% of the reported headline tax gap of 585 million € during 2011–2014 can be regarded as being associated with "anything resembling a loophole". Unfortunately, such campaigns have an influence on policymakers as well as tax auditors, and you will always have to be prepared to defend your qualitative assessment (i.e., when the profit allocation within your MNE has elements of a "skewed" distribution, these are the issues you need to focus on when preparing your defense and documentation—see further below).[75]

While the Burberry example can be regarded as an extreme case insofar as emphasizing the value of a brand is concerned, business models which revolve

[74]In the case of Burberry, substantiating the DEMPE functions could be straightforward. In the interest of "smaller" taxpayers, it must be emphasized, however, that the introduction of the DEMPE concept should not be abused by tax authorities to demand excessive additional documentation—the principle of proportionality must be observed. Sometimes it may help to be "extremely" transparent and "vividly."

[75]Please make sure to read Mayas Article; Forstater (2017); it is a must read for anyone interested in participating in the discourse on tax avoidance. I would suggest that respective claims made by NGOs reflect an incomplete understanding of the arm's length principle and economics in general. Their propagation of formulary apportionment, which is based on the belief that value added can be quantified by headcount/tangible assets, and turnover, is clearly the "fatal conceit" in the realm of transfer pricing. Maybe I must apologize. I honestly did my best to constrain myself throughout this book, but at least in this footnote, I want to refer to the political aspects of transfer pricing. The danger that the arm's length principle will be sacrificed (to be replaced by formulary apportionment) for some vague and ill-conceived notion of "fair" taxation that masks a tax-grabbing agenda of the proponents is a very real danger—at least within the EU (think: CCCTB). I devote a substantial part of my time to highlight the dangerous consequences of such irresponsible political propositions and interested readers are invited to check out my quarterly contributions to the Cayman Financial Review in which I comment on related issues. Also, if you have not realized it thus far, this book is a love letter to the arm's length principle. By illustrating the economic foundations of the arm's length principle and by explaining how it can be effectively used to ensure that transfer prices are aligned will value creation, I am hopefully able to show why sustaining the arm's length principle as the international paradigm is a sensible idea.

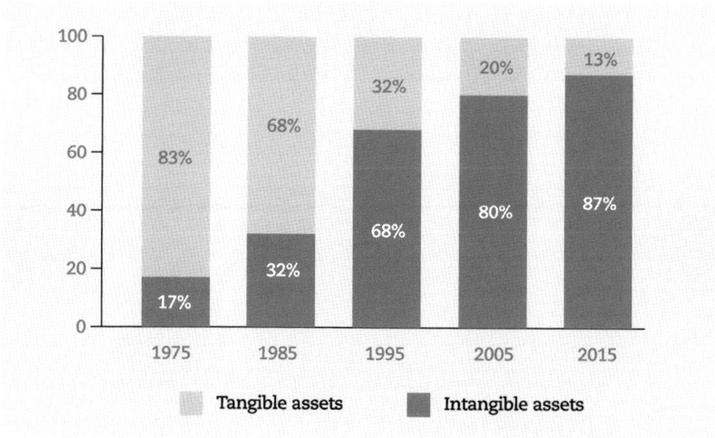

Fig. 3.19 Importance of intangibles (source: Freestone 2018)

around intangibles are the rule rather than the exception. Hence, when embarking on a transfer pricing project, understanding the importance of intangibles should be at the top of your list—for that reason three of the "Key Questions" listed in Annex A are targeted at IP. Figure 3.19 provides a general illustration of the increasing importance of intangibles in the economy—the drastic effect is intended to motivate you to go the extra mile when it comes to analyzing the impact of intangibles on your transfer pricing system.[76]

When quantifying value-added contribution, the effect of intangibles on value creation illustrated above should function as a safeguard and plausibility-check. While a transaction party may perform a wide range of low-value-added routine functions, you must make sure that summing up these individual contributions does not outweigh one or two high-value-added functions that include the contribution of

[76]The illustration stems from a publication of Freestone (2018). Tim actually proceeds to explain that the effect highlighted by the figure can be largely explained by the composition of the S&P 500 and that one should not conclude that the value of commercial property has decreased in absolute terms (nor has it been rendered irrelevant in relative terms). However, I only got to know Tim because he was looking for someone to discuss the effects of BEPS on transparency and disclosure requirements for intangibles. From our discussion, I learned that even for the insurance industry the increased focus on intangibles is relevant. One additional factor to keep in mind in this context is that most of us (me included) tend to have a too narrow understanding of intangibles. In Sections A.3 and A.4 of Chapter VI of the OECD-GL, the OECD has provided an overview of the categories of intangibles. It is extremely helpful to read through these categories to get an understanding and feeling for aspects that merit closer attention in respect to your business model; i.e., one issue you should put on your agenda is to identify your "trade secrets" and think about their impact on your transfer pricing system. Proactively applying the DEMPE concept to identify potential misalignments between economic and legal ownership will be worthwhile for mitigating structural (systemic) transfer pricing risks. These are, however, rather "advanced" transfer pricing questions which will be dealt with in the advanced section of the 2nd volume of this book (if ever. . .).

unique and valuable intangibles. Again, in the case of Burberry, the operative functions and contributions related to retail, logistic, and administration will never outweigh the contributions made by the designer and strategic marketing staff. When applying the arm's length principle, "quality" of contributions matter when assessing the allocation of profits. You cannot substitute quality with quantity—that is not how economics or business work.[77]

Finally, the **PSM decision tree** can be summarized as follows:

1. Did we manage to identify a "clear-cut" tested party?
   (a) If "yes," good => generally no need to look more closely at the PSM.
   (b) If "no" or you were "unsure" => well, go to 2.
2. Are we dealing with a value chain that is highly integrated and features intangibles?
   (a) If "yes," here we go => You will have to carefully look at the PSM—at the very least as a secondary method.
   (b) If "no," fair enough => make sure that none of the "red-flags" triggering the use of the PSM are likely to cause you to lose sleep. Chances are that you will be able to obtain reliable results by applying a different method—you should, however, consider explicitly "rejecting" the applicability of the PSM when compiling your transfer pricing documentation—just to be on the safe side.

Case Study: Can the Prima Group Utilize the Profit Split?

Well, Prima just introduced a target margin (TNMM) based transfer pricing system. So there seems hardly room to apply the PSM. True. Two basic scenarios, however, seem a little plausible:

(a) Prima establishes a subsidiary in Asia and decides to pursue a different business strategy (allocating more functions and risks to the local distributor—compared to the other Prima distributors)

[77]That is why I consider the country-by-country reporting (CbC-R) to be so "dangerous" to the general perception of the arm's length principle. Even though the OECD has consistently rejected formulary apportionment, the introduction of CbC-R is bound to be interpreted (by tax authorities and NGOs—see above) in a way that suggests that only (tangible) quantity should matter and that any deviation is unwarranted. In nothing else, you could even look at the transfer valuations of soccer players—i.e., based on transfermarkt.de, Neymar is valued at €180 Mio., while all 30 players of my beloved hamburger SV are collectively valued at €56 Mio. (in December 2018). That seems about accurate to me. To be sure, there some talented guys on the Hamburger SV squat (Arp and Ito)—but, in the scheme of things (competitive soccer) no one (especially Neymar's club Paris) would trade Neymar for all the Hamburg players. The reason is obvious: all the Hamburg players combined will not help Paris to become more competitive (i.e., win the Champions League). Hence, sticking with the Burberry example, when thinking of calibrating the value-added contributions, think of Neymar (unique and valuable) when valuing strategic decisions and IP, and think of the Hamburger SV when valuing operative functions (low value added and substitutable). This is the last soccer analogy—promise.

(b) Prima merges with a competitor ("Rothwell Gornt") that has a largely complementary product portfolio. The two companies adopt a multiple brand strategy and sustain their brand for their respective legacy businesses. In addition, however, they envision that they can realize synergies by collaboratively developing entirely new line of products which do not cannibalize the legacy business; i.e., they will develop revolutionary "on-board entertainment" (for aircraft and trains). The respective business will be largely project based; i.e., Prima and Rothwell Gornt will jointly acquire projects in the course of which the collaborate to develop and implement customized entertainment solutions.

Scenario (a): Prima Asia as "Super Distributor"

Starting with scenario (a), i.e., Prima Asia, we first have to specify how the different business strategy translates to the functional and risk analysis. So, for the sake of brevity, let's build on the functional and risk analysis established in Sect. 2.2—by adding the new distribution entity (Prima Asia) in the right-hand column of Fig. 3.20. As the functional profile of Prima will be different for transactions with Prima Asia, the adjusted profile is also illustrated on the right-hand side.

What can we conclude at this point? Well, based on the functional and risk profile, it is clear that Prima Asia contributes a substantially higher share of the total value-added as the other Prima subsidiaries. Most notably, Prima Asia assumes critical marketing and sales functions—indicating a comparatively pronounced degree of autonomy for respective strategic decisions on the local market. Prima GmbH will, however, likely sustain all strategic functions relating to global brand strategy and is also likely to perform a wide scope of centralized marketing functions. Assuming that successful marketing of the Prima products requires a highly idiosyncratic marketing strategy and strongly depends on a local network established by the sales personnel, a valuation of the value-added contribution as shown above appears plausible. It also appears plausible that Prima Asia would contribute value by performing some local sourcing and procurement—but the overall value attributable to these functions will likely remain limited. Finally, based on the relevant economic parameters of the case, it would not be plausible for Prima Asia to make material contributions to R&D or production (where would the know-how come from? How could it possibly "stack up" against the intangibles accumulated by Prima?). At most, it seems plausible that Prima Asia would facilitate communications between Prima GmbH research staff and local authorities for purposes of obtaining certificates and meeting other local requirements. Also, the sales personnel of Prima Asia could perform some market research that could be utilized by Prima to optimize product development. In sum, it can certainly be concluded that Prima Asia contributes material value-added and does not exhibit a "routine" functional profile—this conclusion is sufficient for determining that the established target margin system established for the other local Prima distribution entities would not be viable for Prima Asia.

Function	Prima	Subsidiaries	Prima	Prima Asia
Research/Production	+ + + + +		+ + + + +	(+)
Procurement	+ +	+	(+)	+ +
Quality Assurance	+ +	+	+	+ +
Logistics/Warehousing[a]	+ +	+	+	+ +
Sales/Marketing	+ + + +	+ +	+ +	+ + + +
After Sales	+ +	+	(+)	+ +
Management / Administration	+	+	(+)	+
Risks	**Prima**	**Subsidiaries**	**Prima**	**Prima Asia**
Research and Development	+ + + + +		+ + + + +	
Product Liability and Quality	+ +	+	+ +	+
Market Risk	+ + +	+ +	+	+ + +
Customer Credit Risk	+	+		+

Fig. 3.20 Functional and risk profile of Prima Asia

But what is the alternative ? Can we conclude that the PSM constitutes the most reliable method?

The first step should be to assess whether Prima Asia could be identified as the tested party for the controlled transaction (i.e., the sale of Prima Products in Asia)—if so, the resale RPM should still be a viable method. To make a respective assessment, it is now recommended to conduct a quantitative analysis. Figure 3.21 illustrates a respective analysis—utilizing the value chain analysis tool[78] (as we do not have more detailed knowledge of the relevant facts and circumstances, the following is an abbreviated analysis—given the situation at hand, it would be

[78]**The Excel Tool ("Value Chain Analysis") is available in** http://extras.springer.com **for download on the homepage of Transfer Pricing in Lesson** (see also Chapter 2.2).

Selection of relevant processes	value added	Prima	Prima Asia	share of total value added
R&D	18	17.5	0.5	32%
Research	8	100%	0%	14%
Product Development	10	95%	5%	18%
Sub-Process 3	0	100%	0%	0%
Sub-Process 4	0	100%	0%	0%
Production	10	7.6	2.4	18%
Production	6	100%	0%	11%
Quality Assurance	4	40%	60%	7%
Logistics (warehousing)	5	1.8	3.2	9%
Transport (warehousing)	2	30%	70%	4%
Procurement	3	40%	60%	5%
Sales and Marketing	18	6.8	11.2	32%
Sales	10	20%	80%	18%
Marketing	8	60%	40%	14%
Service (After Sales)	4	1.6	2.4	7%
After Sales	4	40%	60%	7%
Administration	1	0.4	0.6	2%
Administration	1	40%	60%	2%
Total	56	35.7	20.3	
Share of Value Added %		64%	36%	
classification of entities		**Entrepreneur**	**Entrepreneur (?)**	

Fig. 3.21 Value chain analysis for Prima Asia (source: own Illustration)

recommended to conduct a more detailed analysis—i.e., using additional sub-functions).

What can we conclude now? Well, we (arguably) now have an analysis which at least approximates the value-added contributions made by the two parties. In sum, and based on the facts and circumstances discussed above, it appears plausible that Prima contributes about two-thirds of the total value added, while prima Asia contributes about one-third. There could certainly be discussions about some of the individual valuations, but the big picture seems clear enough. Prima exclusively performs one of the two main functions (R&D) and also makes substantial contributions to the second core function, i.e., marketing (including valuable intangibles such as the brand as well as strategic decisions and know-how). Prima Asia on the other hand does make valuable contributions to the core functions of sales and marketing (including some local intangibles) but, considering the entire value chain for the controlled transactions, exhibits a less pronounced functional profile. I would argue that the classification of Prima Asia is a tricky task—it is somewhere between a "strong" routine entity ("routine plus") and a weak (local) entrepreneur. While Prima Asia, acting as a reseller, would thus be likely to qualify as tested party, it is not "clear-cut." Looking back at the PSM decision tree, it would thus be prudent to move from 1b to 2b scenario (2.a. would be rejected because the degree of integration, looking at dominance of the retail functions, cannot be considered "high"). Following the advice for a 2.b. scenario, we should thus review the red flags for triggering a PSM:

- Are we looking at a situation in which multiple parties make important contributions to key value-added functions, which cannot appropriately (easily) be segmented? *No, the value chain is characterized by sequential inputs that can mostly be segmented.*

- Do multiple parties contribute (unique and valuable) intangibles? *Not really, the intangibles contributed by Prima Asia are not really considered unique and valuable—and are certainly subordinated to the contributions made by Prima*
- The business model is focused on exploiting IP (with one entity permitting a related party to use of a brand or technological know-how)? *Yes. Essentially,* Prima Asia utilizes *the IP of Prima to make sales throughout Asia.*
- Are we dealing with a project-based business model? *No.*

Based on this high-level analysis, we would likely not lose too much sleep over the red flags. Especially when looking at the third-bullet, we find ourselves in a situation in which it is possible that third parties would regard Prima Asia is primarily as a reseller/distributor utilizing the brand that lacks the degree of autonomy usually attributed to a licensee of franchisee[79]—hence, it appears more plausible (and feasible) to apply the RPM and conceive the resale margin as a compensation for the value-added by the functions performed by Prima Asia. At some point, we must decide. In the case at hand, based on the known facts, the PSM is unlikely to yield the most reliable results and should not be selected as the applicable transfer pricing method, at least not as a primary method. I would venture to suggest that applying the PSM would not be entirely absurd and that outright rejecting it may not be straightforward. Ultimately, the argument would mostly have to be based on the lack of a high level of integration and also emphasize that the intangibles contributed by Prima Asia may not be considered as being unique and valuable.

Prima Asia could essentially be termed (classified) as a "super distributor" compared to the Prima distributors operating in Europe or North America. While Prima Asia performs more extensive functions and has a high degree of autonomy, Prima headquarters will still act as the principal. Hence, at the end of the day, Prima Asia seems to be (much) closer to being classified as a distributor than a (local) entrepreneur. Possibly, the easiest (most pragmatic) option would be to integrate Prima Asia in the existing transfer pricing system by applying a (substantially) extended target range—here, it would also be highly recommended to compile a benchmark study with local comparables which could also be calibrated to account for the more pronounced functional profile (applying different criteria and thresholds compared to the European benchmark discussed above).

The PSM could, arguably, be utilized as a secondary (validation mechanism). It will, however, be an operative challenge to accurately determine the "profits to be split"—as this will require a segmented cost accounting for Prima for activities

[79]The application of a CUP (license benchmark) as well as the application of rules of thumb to evaluate the arm's length nature of license arrangement will be illustrated in Annex C—as a variation to the case study presented here. In that case, Prima Asia will be assumed to have a substantially higher degree of autonomy and that the transfer price (license fee) is a compensation for the use IP (know-how, brand) contributed by Prima rather than a remuneration for the functions performed by Prima Asia. Naturally, the application of the PSM would also be more plausible in this scenario—but due to the low degree of integration, it would arguably still not constitute the most reliable method.

Prima Asia	2019 (FC)	2020 (FC)	2021 (FC)	Total	Average
Revenues	8,000,000 €	15,000,000 €	25,000,000 €	48,000,000 €	16,000,000 €
COGS	6,000,000 €	11,250,000 €	18,750,000 €	36,000,000 €	12,000,000 €
Gross Margin (%)	25.0%	25.0%	25.0%	25.0%	25.0%
OPEX	3,000,000 €	4,500,000 €	5,000,000 €	12,500,000 €	4,166,667 €
EBIT	−1,000,000 €	−750,000 €	1,250,000 €	−500,000 €	−166,667 €
Net Margin (%)	−12.5%	−5.0%	5.0%	−1.0%	−1.0%

Fig. 3.22 P&L forecast for Prima Asia (source: own Illustration)

relating to the business in Asia; i.e., the respective costs would have to be delineated from costs incurred in the relation to the other Prima sales entities as well as from Prima's business on its local market[80].

Let's finally look at some financial data as well. Figure 3.22 illustrates a forecast (business) case for the Prima Asia—based on the MPL minus 25% pricing that is established for transactions with the other sales entities (a rather likely approach for an initial forecast—the nice way of putting it is "we are all susceptible to the anchoring bias"—well and sometimes a tad bit lazy).

So, how would we comment on this forecast as the in-house transfer pricing department? Well, considering that Prima Asia—being classified as a sort of "super distributor"—(almost) achieves a break even position after 3 years, the forecast arguably doesn't quite ring alarm bells. If, feasible one could propose to apply MPL minus 30% for the initial 3 years, which (ceteris paribus) would yield a total EBIT of 1,900,000 and an EBIT % of 4%—not too bad. As pointed out above, management will likely have to be harassed to engage in an active monitoring and adjustment process—but those are the perks of working in a tax department.[81] But, at the end of the day, we could feel sufficiently confident that applying the modified RPM (with an extended target range) will not be entirely wrong.

[80]As the activities of Prima in relation to Prima Asia would likely not be recorded on separate cost centers (i.e., there is likely no (limited)staff specifically dedicated to the business in Asia at the level of Prima), application of the PSM will not be straightforward—if used for validation purposes, a reasonable level of approximation might be sufficient, but this little "detour" perhaps clarifies that applying the PSM as the primary method for the tested transaction here is not considered ideal.

[81]Make no mistake, consultants also tend to be frustrated by a lack of commitment of management to adopt a proactive stance on margin monitoring—we will generally have an easier time shrugging it off though.

Selection of relevant processes	value added	Prima	Prima Asia	share of total value added
R&D	24	10.4	13.6	45%
Research	8	50%	50%	15%
Product Development	8	50%	50%	15%
Design Customization	8	30%	70%	15%
Sub-Process 4	0	100%	0%	0%
Production (implementation)	12	5.4	6.6	23%
Implementation	6	40%	60%	11%
Quality Assurance	6	50%	50%	11%
Logistics (warehousing)	3	1.1	1.9	6%
Transport (warehousing)	1	30%	70%	2%
Procurement	2	40%	60%	4%
Sales and Marketing	9	4.8	4.2	17%
Sales	6	50%	50%	11%
Marketing	3	60%	40%	6%
Service (After Sales)	4	1.2	2.8	8%
After Sales	4	30%	70%	8%
Administration	1	0.4	0.6	2%
Administration	1	40%	60%	2%
Total	53	23.3	29.7	
Share of Value Added %		44%	56%	
classification of entities		Entrepreneur	Entrepreneur	

Fig. 3.23 Value chain analysis for P-RG business (Source: own illustration)

Scenario (b): Merger with Rothwell Gornt

Now, looking at the second variant of the case study, the "merger" with Rothwell Gornt and the pursuit of joint business opportunity ("on-board entertainment") bring us to a plain vanilla-type PSM application. The essence of the case is that two entrepreneurs jointly develop entirely new products which do not cannibalize the legacy business. In the case at hand, it is conceivable that these products will be marketed under a new brand (perhaps—"P-RG Entertainment"). It is also likely that the target customers (i.e., Lufthansa, American Airlines, or large railway operations) have neither been previous customers of either Prima or Rothwell Gornt. Further, plausible, assumptions would be that the two related companies (employees of the separate legacy businesses) will each contribute unique and valuable know-how to each project and that the collaboration will be highly integrated throughout the entire projects, starting from joint acquisitions and pitches to joint design and implementation phases.

Obviously, the setup is calibrated in a way that contains all the red flags for triggering the PSM.[82] Figure 3.23 shows an exemplary value chain analysis for the P-RG business. Compared to the legacy business of Prima, the focus in this b-2-b business is much more focused on R&D and less on marketing. While the inputs contributed by the two parties are not 50%/50% for each main function within the value chain, the project-based business is clearly characterized by a high degree of (parallel) integration.

Based on the analysis, it would certainly seem plausible to allocate the profits according to the ratio resulting from the above calculations. There are, however,

[82] I will admit that joint projects are arguably the single most sensible transaction for the application of the PSM. Also, from a customer's perspective, I would be quite enamored with better on-board entertainment.

some pragmatic aspects that should be considered: (A) any value chain analysis will be subject to a certain degree of "fuzziness." The result shown above is very close to 50%/50%, i.e., it is very close to an "intuitive" split (agreement) between two parties that can be considered equal partners, and tax authorities are likely to accept such a split. (B) When designing the transfer pricing system for the P-RG business, the determined ratio is likely to have the character of a "baseline scenario"; in other words, it is very likely that most projects will have certain particularities deviating from this baseline (short-term variants), and it is also conceivable that, as the business matures, the distribution of value contributions will evolve (long-term effects). Hence, it would be advisable to merely define the baseline scenario as a "starting point" for internal negotiations but allow for deviations—these, however, should be meticulously documented. The advantage here is that you would have a consistent system in place which eliminates systemic risks while also allowing for a high level of flexibility.

Box 3.4 Restating the Lesson

Internal Negotiations Are Great for Approximating an Arm's Length Allocation of Profits => Provided that the Negotiations Are "Real"

The PSM is an important method. By conducting a thorough (quantitative) value chain analysis, you can ensure that the essential features of the tested transaction (business relationship) are accurately captured. The analysis will give you a good idea about the proportion of the value contributions made by individual parties. In cases where the identification of a "tested party" is difficult (subject to potential challenges), applying the PSM as a secondary method to validate the arm's length nature of the profit allocation resulting from the application of other (one-sided) methods.

Also, there are several aspects which would render the PSM to be the most appropriate method for a specific transaction, namely, in case that both (multiple) parties contribute unique and valuable IP and the value chain is highly integrated. The greatest advantage of the PSM is that it is extremely flexible; i.e., it can be applied to virtually all transactions and business models. While the analysis is inevitably based on subjective valuations, the resulting profit allocation will generally be rather balanced (compared to one-sided methods which allocate the residual profits/losses to one party).

For economists, the implied bargaining situation of the PSM is arguably much preferable to comparability analysis based on databases; i.e., instead of having to content with constraints in comparability criteria (often due to a lack of available data), the economist can determine all required parameters for applying the PSM without relying on external data.

While the issue of comparability will thus not impede the application of the PSM, the core task of the economist is to formulate plausible working assumptions regarding the bargaining situation. Each assumption needs to be

(continued)

Box 3.4 (continued)
transparent and well documented—the same applies to the quantitative valuations. A conscientious application of the PSM will greatly enhance the defensibility of the transfer prices in a tax audit. Ideally, tax auditors should be forced to engage on the basis of the economic facts, and it should be clear that any challenges based on a formulary apportionment approach (i.e., based on CbC data) are grossly inferior to a PSM based on a simulated bargaining situation when determining an arm's length allocation of profits. As economists, we need to stress this aspect as much as possible, as it highlights the feasibility of ensuring a "fair" allocation of profits (i.e., ensure that tax avoidance is eliminated) by appropriately applying the arm's length principle.

This also applies for an increasingly digitalized and IP heavy economy. The key to a sustainable international consensus on taxation is to ensure that the stakeholders appreciate the strength of the arm's length principle and feel comfortable with the application and results. What we do not need is ever stricter regulation—or a paradigm shift (to formulary apportionment) that would dissolve the link between economic activity and taxation on the basis of individual business relationships, spawning an unforeseeable extent of conflicts between taxpayers and tax authorities as well as among different tax authorities.

3.5 The Cost Plus Method (C+)

The C+ method (see Fig. 3.24) is conceptually very close to the TNMM (see Sect. 2.3)—at least when applied on a full-cost basis and when calculating the PLI based on an unsegmented P&L. The C+ method can be labeled as the "workhorse" among the transfer pricing methods.[83] This status of the C+ method is also reflected by the fact that a cost + 5% type of remuneration is arguably the single most frequently adopted transfer pricing solution on a global scale—which is also reflected by its status as a "safe harbor" rule for low-value-added services ("LVAS") as introduced by the OECD in 2017 (see further below).

The core issue, or better first and foremost task, when applying the C+ method is applying the lesson of establishing an adequate level of segmentation for your transaction. Analogous to the TNMM, it is vital to clarify the economic nature of

[83]The cost plus method is arguably somewhat more complex than is reflected in this chapter. The discussion here is strongly focused on applying the cost plus method on a net margin basis—when applied on a gross margin basis, application will be much more difficult—as indicated below. In respect to the terminology, I deliberately refrain from differentiating between different variants or sub-categories) of the cost plus method (i.e., CPLUS vs. SCM), adopting C+ method as a kind of umbrella category instead—I hope for readers based in the USA this method of presentation will be sufficiently clear (thanks to Prof. Eden for pointing out the need for clarification on the terminology applied).

OECD Guidelines 2017, Paragraph 2.45

The cost plus method **begins with the costs incurred by the supplier of property (or services)** in a controlled transaction for property transferred or services provided to an associated purchaser. **An appropriate cost plus mark-up is then added to this cost**, to make an appropriate profit in **light of the functions performed and the market conditions**. What is arrived at after adding the cost plus mark up to the above costs may be regarded as an arm's length price of the original controlled transaction.

Fig. 3.24 Cost plus method (source: OECD)

the tested (controlled) transaction. In a situation in which one entity engages in no other activities other than rendering low-value-added (supporting) services to one (or multiple) related party, there is hardly any need to discuss the composition of the cost base. You will, as a general rule, have to include virtually all costs incurred by the entity rendering the services. As the service provider has virtually no additional income (revenue streams) other than the service fee (remuneration) charged to the service recipient(s), such an entity will have no realistically available alternatives to cover any "additional costs," i.e., costs not included in the applied cost base. Such a situation is often encountered when dealing with contract manufacturing or contract R&D arrangements, where the service provider exclusively renders intra-group services (as rendering services to external parties is often undesirable due to strategic objectives). The business set-up in such arrangements is characterized by the service recipient factually determining the scope and the quality of services and having almost unlimited access to information (cost accounting of the service provider) and the ability to monitor the operational and management structure of the service provider (with the local head of operations regularly reporting to the (some) centralized department at the level of the service recipient). Under such a set-up, the service provider may have a lot of leeway in structuring the operational processes, he will, however, have no influence over the ultimate commercialization of his contributions which is at the sole discretion of the service recipient, who, as the principal, will determine the desired capacity and bear the respective market risks. When talking about "costs" relating to such "simple" (routine) kind of services, we should thus understand that, from a transfer pricing perspective, "actual cost" are the relevant basis for evaluating the arm's length nature of the markup. The economic rationale is straightforward; when you engage a service provider to render a specified amount of customized services, the remuneration payable to the service provider cannot depend on your ability to utilize the received services (i.e., integrate the services as a component in your own value creation process) and to ultimately realize a profit. Naturally, any service provider needs to meet the agreed quality criteria and is responsible (and bear the corresponding risk) for failures and inefficiencies within his operating processes. Ultimately, the service provider will, however, be (mostly) isolated from market risks (i.e., from the commercial success of the principal).

When being strict in applying this basic tenet of the C+ method, one can greatly reduce the perceived complexity in transfer pricing structures. Many internal business relationships will qualify for applying the C+ method on a "full" and "actual" cost basis—which is by far the easiest transfer pricing arrangement that, if appropriately applied, will be mostly immune to challenges by tax authorities. When being brutally honest, the degree of authority of entities performing contract manufacturing or contract R&D activities is simply limited. Still, a frequent obstacle to applying the C+ method on the basis of full and actual costs is that, from a management perspective, it is often perceived that the "guaranteed" remuneration would destroy the incentivizing effects of the transfer prices. Hence, management will often favor a more complex price-setting arrangement based on either budgeted (planned or normal) or partial costs. From a business perspective, such price-setting procedures are often sensible and will facilitate efficient processes (if calibrated appropriately). There are, however, two key issues that management should acknowledge before rejecting the application of the C+ method based on actual and full costs:

- *Actual vs. standard costs*: Applying a one-size-fits all transfer price in the form of "normal" or "standard" costs on a global scale will penalize/reward service providers for economic effects that are beyond their "sphere of influence"; i.e., the respective results/effects are not related to the quality of the services rendered. In such cases, the transfer prices will have a dis-incentivizing effect. The inevitable effect is that the respective MNE will have functionally homogeneous service providers (often contract manufacturers) that exhibit highly heterogeneous profit levels (and frequently losses) that persist over a multiple-year period. In these unfortunate cases management needs to acknowledge that it is time to abolish the one-size-fits all price-setting as it makes little economic sense. While it would not be required to directly apply actual costs, management would have to introduce a "modification factor" for the standard costs[84] which ensures that the structural advantages/disadvantages leading to the persistence of extreme results is eliminated (minimized).
- *Full vs. partial costs*[85]: If deviating from a full-costs approach, the applied markup would, ceteris paribus, have to be higher to enable the service provider to cover its costs and to realize a net margin that is commensurate with its functional and risk analysis. In other words, the composition of the cost base cannot be calibrated in such a way that the service provider is, despite adequate performance, persistently unable to cover the costs and realize an arm's length profits. When excluding costs from the costs base (costs above EBT) while

[84]To be clear, applying standardized costs reflects arm's length behavior and is thus appropriate from a transfer pricing perspective. The OECD emphasizes that "Associated enterprises may choose to calculate their cost plus basis on a standardized basis. An independent party probably would not accept to pay a higher price resulting from the inefficiency of the other party. On the other hand, if the other party is more efficient than can be expected under normal circumstances, this other party should benefit from that advantage. The associated enterprise may agree in advance which costs would be acceptable as a basis for the cost plus method." Please note that it is made very clear by the OECD that the variations in price (remuneration) must be due to the efficiency (performance) of the service provider—i.e., there is no legitimation of one-size-fits all standard costs.

[85]The OECD differentiates between (1) direct, (2) indirect, and (3) overhead costs—acknowledging, however, that it is difficult to accurately delineate these costs (see OECD-GL 2017a, Paragraph 2.53) and that ultimately the relevant economic discussion boils down to the gross profit vs. net profit analysis (see OECD-GL 2017a, Paragraph 2.53).

refusing to increase the markup, management should explain how the service provider is expected to cover these costs.

The mechanics and implementations of these issues are eerily similar to those elaborated in the context of the modified RPM (see above)—which, considering that in both cases we are focused on determining an arm's length compensation for a tested party, should not be entirely surprising.

While applying the C+ method on the basis of actual and full costs is comparatively easy (i.e., there is a reason why the C+ method is the workhorse of transfer pricing), it becomes much more challenging when applied to more complex cases.[86] Paragraphs 2.52–2.58 of the OECD-GL (2017a), which deal with the application of the C+ method, are arguably among the most difficult and abstract explanations of a transfer pricing method contained in the entire guidelines. The following bullet points provide a non-exhaustive (i.e., blatantly ignoring the more complex issues such as how to interpret "marginal costs" or "historical costs" in a transfer pricing context) compilation of issues you should be aware of when applying the C+ method:

- It is strongly recommended to compile a contractual basis, which includes a clear delineation of the scope of services as well as a definition of the applicable cost base. A respective written agreement should be considered "a MUST." Please never enter a tax audit without having appropriate contracts in place—there is simply no conceivable reason to shirk this comparatively minor effort. The contract should also clarify and specify the rights and obligations of the parties, with the primary intent being to illustrate and substantiate the routine classification of the service provider.[87] In this context, it is also important to ensure that the contractual allocation of risks is commensurate with the functional and risk profile of the transacting parties, i.e.,
  - The routine nature of contract manufacturing activities should be complemented by the "guarantee" of the service recipient to purchase all respective products over an adequate span of time (budget period), as the contract manufacturer will have factually no opportunity to market any excess (see above).
  - The routine nature of a contract researcher will most clearly be reflected in the fact that the contract researcher will be remunerated irrespective of the

[86]While the TNMM evolves more or less fluently into the modified RPM when complexity increases, the application of the C+ method will demand a much higher attention to the issue of "comparability" (and performing respective adjustment calculations as well as adequately segmenting the applicable cost base).

[87]One crucial element in this context is to integrate a provision that clarifies that all relevant (unique and valuable) IP is owned by the service recipient (and that ownership will be retained throughout the duration of the business relationship and beyond).

subsequent commercialization; i.e., the principal will be entitled to all entrepreneurial profits and needs to bear all respective risks.[88]

- Differences in the level and types of expenses—operating expenses and non-operating expenses including financing expenditures—must be appropriately considered[89] (see OECD-GL, Paragraph 2.51) in the context of the comparability analysis. With respect to financing expenditure, you need to ensure that the interest expenses incurred by the service provider do not cannibalize the remuneration earned from rendering the services; i.e., a third-party service provider would not commit to render services to a principal if he were to incur interest expenses (for procuring the required production capacity) that exceed the potential profit to be earned form the business relationship.[90]
- The composition of the cost base will need to differentiate between different kind of costs; i.e., costs not reflecting (relating to) a value-added activity should not be subjected to a(n) (equal) markup. The same would generally have to apply for "pass-through" costs as well as for costs relating to overhead expenses originally incurred at the level of the principal (often centralized services, such as IT services[91]).

The less then optimal (inconclusive and ambiguous) guidance provided by the OECD translates into substantial uncertainty when applying the C+ method outside of the context of routine services, i.e., services that can be remunerated on full and

[88]In this context, it is also crucial to observe OECD-GL Paragraph 2.49 according to which "[. . .] there are other circumstances where there is no discernible link between the level of costs incurred and a market price (e.g. where a valuable discovery has been made and the owner has incurred only small research costs in making it)." Hence, it is crucial to clearly delineate ownership of IP (see previous footnote) for avoiding any discussions with tax authorities relating to the allocation of the residual (entrepreneurial) profits.

[89]In this context, the OECD particularly stresses the need for appropriate segmentation; i.e., you would have to be careful not to utilize the unsegmented P&L to determine the (full) cost base when a Contract Manufacturer renders additional or complementary services. In some sense this is similar to appropriately distinguishing between resale and commission business when calculating the PLI—see above). Specifically, the OECD highlights that "[. . .] separate compensation for those functions may need to be determined. Such functions may for example amount to the provision of services for which an appropriate reward may be determined."

[90]Note: If the service provider renders services in the exclusive interest of one service recipient, it is economically sensible (from the perspective of the service recipient) to perceive the required financing (loan) for procuring the required productive capacity as a precondition for obtaining the services. Hence, an independent business manager could reasonably be expected to consent advancing the financing without (or at minimal) interest. Considering that a loan (as well as the sale or lease of machinery) would clearly be of supportive and complementary nature to the services, the aggregation would be commensurate with the principles outlined above). So, you would generally not have to conduct a benchmark for the loan—as a CUP will likely not be appropriate in these circumstances (i.e., the loan is advanced in the context of a highly idiosyncratic business relationship and is thus not readily comparable to interest rates observed on the financial markets).

[91]See OECD-GL (2017a), Paragraph 2.56.

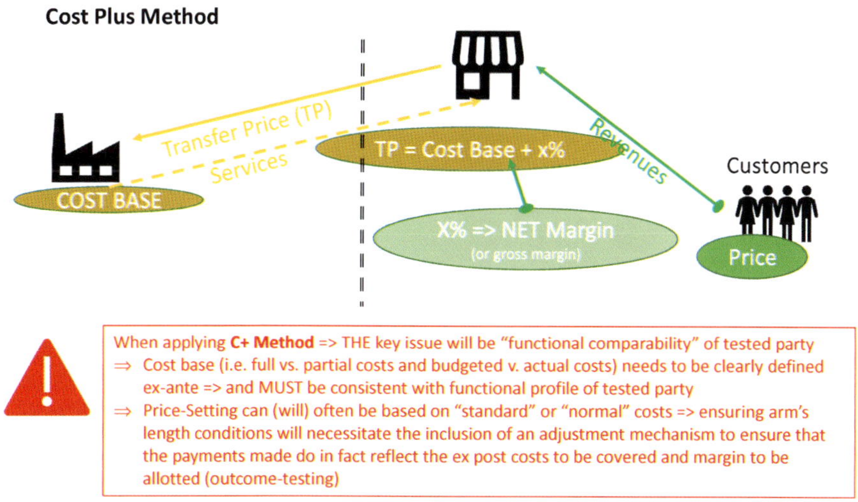

Fig. 3.25 Applying the cost plus method (Source: own illustration)

actual costs and centralized services (see below). This may be a surprising statement, but considering that the C+ method is in most cases applied analogously to the TNMM (either intentionally or unintentionally), this issue has not received all that much attention.[92] You should not be discouraged, however, as most transactions will qualify for the application of the C+ method on the basis of "full" and "actual" costs (see above)—culminating in a comparability analysis based on the net profitability of the service provider.

Figure 3.25 summarizes the basics of the C+ method (tested party acting as a service provider rendering contract manufacturing or research services).

Considering the foregoing, the <u>**C+ method decision tree**</u> is rather sparse and can be summarized as follows:

1. Did we manage to identify a "clear-cut" tested party (ideally – providing routine services)?

   (a) If "yes", excellent => we should apply the C+ method on the basis of full and actual costs => i.e., in the context of an analysis of the net profitability of the service provider (the respective analytical steps are akin to those for the TNMM and the modified RPM, including the alignment between price-setting and outcome-testing perspective).

[92]Note: This applies also in the context of the BEPS project—where, among the transfer pricing methods, the focus was on the PSM. The C+ method was only (peripherally) discussed in the context of LVAS (see below). For what it is worth, one may conclude that C+ method based transfer pricing systems are not prone to come under BEPS-motivated scrutiny of tax authorities. While there may be some merit to such a conclusion, it is quite dangerous. In practice, tax authorities (esp. in Germany) will regularly review the applied cost base and do not hesitate to challenge individual costs (especially if the cost base is not appropriately defined in a respective contract).

   (b) If "no" or you were "unsure" => double- and triple-check (seriously). Fight for a strict application of the basic tenant of the C+ method (i.e., isolating the service provider from market risk). If management refuses to listen => well, go to Step 2), but emphasize that, at least for outcome-testing purposes, the actual net results (losses or high profits) of the service provider cannot be completely disregarded without incurring substantial tax risks due to transfer pricing adjustments (at least so long as service provider is not an entrepreneur). Also, when going to Step 2, you should automatically start to think about applying alternative or secondary methods.

2. Are we dealing with a service provider (internal supplier) which either possesses substantial intangibles or which pursues complex business activities (including direct relationships with external parties)?

   (a) If "yes," well you have to dig deep => In the first step, you will have to accurately delineate the different transactions => in the second step, you will have to analyze the comparable transactions (here: internal comparables) => if feasible, depending on the functional profile of the service provider, you should aim to substantiate your analysis based on internal comparables with a benchmark (net profitability). Also, the PSM could be utilized as a secondary method (validate the arm's length nature of the profit allocation)—here the strength of the PSM can be harnessed, i.e., preventing an extremely skewed" or one-sided profit allocation.
   (b) If "yes," you are actually looking at the headquarters of the MNE => look also at the services recipient. There is a good chance that you need to adopt a more holistic (aggregated) approach to evaluate the arm's length nature of prices for the services in the context of the business relationship.
   (c) If "no," => please adhere to the strict application of the basic tenant of the C + method—as outlined above.

Case Study: Why Would the Prima Group Utilize the Cost Plus Method?
Based on the facts and circumstances established above, there is little need to apply the C+ method for transactions between Prima and the international subsidiaries, expect for the provision of centralized services which will be discussed in the "Advanced" section (see Sec. 4 below). Considering that the international subsidiaries of Prima perform routine distribution functions, the TNMM and modified RPM offer a better fit to the business model than the C+ method.

Above, I have complained about the guidance for applying the C+ method contained in the paragraphs 2.52–2.58 of the OECD-GL (2017a). Unfortunately, the first of the three examples for application of the C+ method provided in paragraphs 2.59–2.61 of the OECD-GL (2017a) also exhibits several shortcomings. This case study will review these examples by "translating" them into "proposals" made by the Prima management and formulating some of-the-cuff responses (indicative evaluation) from the perspective of the transfer pricing department.

Manufacturing (Non-routine) (Based on OECD-GL 2017a, Paragraph 2.59)

Prima Management: "When selling our products to our foreign subsidiaries, we earn a 5% gross profit mark up with respect to its manufacturing operation (evidenced by our internal controlling and accounting data). Based on available market analysis we have identified that X, Y, and Z are independent domestic manufacturers of comparable products which sell to independent foreign purchasers. The available data shows that X, Y, and Z earn gross profit mark-ups with respect to their manufacturing operations that range from 3% to 5%. We have further identified that our controlling accounts for supervisory, general, and administrative costs as operating expenses, and thus these costs are not reflected in cost of goods sold. The gross profit mark ups of X, Y, and Z, however, reflect supervisory, general, and administrative costs as part of the costs of goods sold. Therefore, the gross profit mark ups of X, Y, and Z must be adjusted (increased) to provide accounting consistency. Can you please make a recommendation of how to ensure of transfer prices comply with arm's length conditions?"

Response(s) from TP Perspective: "It seems questionable that our manufacturing operation can be adequately isolated from the other functions performed at headquarter level (i.e. research, marketing) from an economic perspective. Prima, as the entrepreneur of our Group, engages in a wide range of value-added functions which are closely intertwined. Hence, it will generally not be appropriate to identify Prima as the 'tested party' for the sale of products to our foreign subsidiaries—as this would contradict the functional and risk profile of the entities. The arm's length nature of the transfer prices agreed between Prima and our foreign subsidiaries can thus not be ensured by applying the C+ method—even for the application as a secondary method (validation or plausibility check) the C+ method cannot be regarded as suitable. Furthermore, it appears highly questionable whether the identified 'peer group' (X, Y, Z) would be adequate comparables—it appears likely that these companies will pursue different business strategies and it will (frankly) be unfeasible to make accurate adjustments for the accounting differences (i.e. we will not be able to reliably 'equalize' the cost of goods sold). In sum, we strongly recommend reassessing whether the gross profit mark-up earned is a suitable basis for determining our transfer pricing policy."

Manufacturing (Routine) (Based on OECD-GL 2017a, Paragraph 2.60)

Prima Management: "As you know, the company Havergill Products located in Tanzania is a 100% subsidiary of Prima. In comparison with Germany, wages are very low in Tanzania. Based on the transfer pricing system implemented by your predecessor, television sets are assembled by Havergill products at the expense and risk of Prima. All the necessary components, know-how, etc. are naturally provided by Prima. The purchase of the assembled product is guaranteed by Prima in case the television sets meet a certain quality standard.[93] After the quality check, the

[93] Note: In the OECD example, the case states: " [. . .] The purchase of the assembled product is guaranteed by Prima in case the television sets fail to meet a certain quality standard." I suggest that the "fail to" is a plain mistake and should be corrected. Obviously, the contract manufacturer will

television sets are brought—at the expense and risk of Prima—to distribution centers Prima has established in several countries. The function of Havergill Products can be described as a purely contract manufacturing function. The risks Havergill Products could bear are eventual differences in the agreed quality and quantity. The basis for applying the cost plus method will be formed by all the costs connected to the assembling activities. The applied mark-up is 5%. Do you see any transfer pricing related risks?"

Response(s) from TP Perspective: "Based on the big picture, the transfer pricing structure between Prima and Havergill Products indeed reflects a fairly simple contract manufacturing arrangement and seems to be commensurate with the functional and risk profile of both parties. Havergill Products exhibits the characteristics of a routine entity and is the obvious choice as a tested party. Considering that it is questionable that we will be able to identify a sufficient number of local comparables for the tested party in commercial databases, we need to address the question of whether 'comparability' adjustments are required to account for specific market conditions; specifically, we will have to assess whether the 5% mark-up adequately reflects the economic rationale in an arm's length context. The core issue here is to determine whether the local wage structure constitutes a 'location specific advantage' (so-called LSA). While the OECD is very clear in pointing out that LSAs are not capable of being owned or controlled, and therefore not regarded as intangibles, they should, however, be considered in a comparability analysis. In the case of Havergill Products it must be assessed whether at arm's length, the management of Havergill Products would be content with a comparatively small cost mark up of 5%, which, while being almost a default (or factual safe harbor) in Europe, may be considered insufficient by tax authorities of countries exhibiting respective market characteristics. In the absence of adequate local comparables, we must thus be careful when determining the cost mark-up—while this is not a 'systemic risk', respective challenges by the local authorities can still be rather aggressive, with the demanded mark-up often approaching or exceeding 20%.[94] It is thus recommended to proactively address the following questions (see OECD-GL, Paragraph 1.140ff.); (i) do location savings exist? (ii) what is the amount of any location savings? (iii) what is the extent to which location savings are passed on to independent customers or suppliers; and (iv) where location savings are not fully passed on to independent

---

have to comply to the defined quality criteria to earn the agreed remuneration—failure to comply with the defined standard operating procedures as well as gross negligence or willful misconduct will reduce the remuneration of the contract manufacturer; i.e., as in any arm's length situation, the principal will not make (full) payments to a service provider that is not complying with the agreed procedures.

[94]In day-to-day practice, such comments would primarily be targeted at China or India. Both countries have clarified their respective positions in the context of the UN guidance for transfer pricing. As the availability of local comparables is continually improving for these countries, taxpayers should look into conducting local benchmarks—here the trade-off of spending money on such a study is generally favorable. Also, the respective analysis not only is suitable for ensuring local compliance but will also help to defend higher margins vis-à-vis the European tax authority.

customers or suppliers, what is the manner in which independent enterprises operating under similar circumstances would allocate any retained net location savings?"

Research and Development (Routine) (Based on OECD-GL 2017a, Paragraph 2.61)

Prima Management: "Travkin Labs, a 100% subsidiary of Prima based in Russia, agrees to carry out contract research for Prima. All risks related to the research shall be assumed by company Prima. The agreement clarifies that Prima also owns all the intangibles developed through the research and therefore has also the profit chances resulting from the research. We understand that this is a typical setup for applying a cost plus method. All costs for the research, which the associated parties have agreed upon, have to be compensated. The additional cost plus may reflect how innovative and complex the research carried out is. Please asses the tax viability and outline the most important contractual provisions."

Response(s) from TP Perspective: "The tax viability of the outlined transfer pricing arrangement can be evaluated as high. Depending on the nature of the research, the cost plus could exceed 5%; i.e. be oriented toward the upper bound of an applicable arm's length range.[95] There will, however, be a natural ceiling determined by the routine classification of Travkin Labs. In terms of the most important contractual provisions, it should be clearly stipulated that Travkin Labs will be remunerated irrespective of whether the research results in marketable products. Such a provision will be vital to substantiate the routine classification of Travkin Labs. To avoid principal agent problems, the respective provisions should be complemented with stipulations regarding agreed standard procedures, budgetary oversight and other monitoring provisions. It should also be understood that to adequately comply with the post-BEPS regulations, care should be taken to define the contributions and obligations of the principal (Prima). Specific attention should be paid to appropriately aligning the performance of the DEMPE functions between Prima and Travkin Labs."

[95]The above comments for LSA's should be observed in the context of Russia as well.

Box 3.5 Restating the Lesson

Arm's Length Net Margins Should Make Everyone Happy—Part 2

If the TNMM is not primarily about net margins or benchmarking, but rather about conducting a solid functional and risk analysis, the same applies to the C+ method. A clandestine classification of the tested party as a "routine entity" will enable you to apply a straightforward analysis based on actual and full costs. Again, once it is agreed that the tested party does not make unique and valuable contributions, it should also automatically be agreed that a remuneration that ensures small but stable profits will reflect arm's length conditions.

The C+ method can also be reliably applied in cases where the tested party does not exhibit a routine profile and thus conceptionally allows for a higher degree of flexibility compared to the TNMM. In such cases, the cost basis will often deviate from full and actual costs, and the price-setting will focus on a gross margin. In such cases, the arm's length nature of the resulting profit allocation can often be substantiated by applying secondary methods (PSM or internal comparables). It will be essential (as emphasized in the context of the RPM) to realize that the transfer pricing analysis will have to extend beyond the gross margin and ultimately consider the business relationship as a whole. In other words, one-size-fits-all approaches based on standard costs applied globally will likely not be feasible due to differences in local market conditions or cost structures.

The bottom line is the following: While an internal service provider does not need to be excluded from all economic risks, it must be ensured that only such risks will have an effect on the results of the service provider which can be directly influenced by the personnel performing the service functions. While a service provider will thus be responsible for efficiently performing the assigned functions, he can only bear market risks to the extent to which he can reasonable expected to adjust his capacity or independently market products to external customers.

Chapter 4
Applying the Lesson to More Complex Transactions

Having reached this stage of the book, it should have become clear that applying the arm's length principle is not some dark science practice by MNEs to avoid paying taxes. The case studies of the Prima Group were intended to demonstrate that the art of transfer pricing consists in finding an appropriate balance between the business and the tax considerations by avoiding the myopia of a fragmented transaction-by-transaction type of analysis, i.e., being mindful of the economic essence of the business relationship as a whole. We have also gained a pragmatic understanding of the available tools (transfer pricing methods) available for applying the lesson for a wide range of intra-group business relations.

As stated in the Introduction, my hope and intention in writing this book was to equip the "beginner" (i.e., young transfer pricing professionals, in-house tax staff (partially) assigned to transfer pricing, as well as students) with pragmatic guidance for their first steps into the realm of transfer pricing. I sincerely hope that the guidance is suitable to bolster their confidence in applying the arm's length principle. As it was never my intention to write a tome-like reference book dealing with all conceivable transfer pricing aspects for all types of transactions, the book could arguably end right here. The lesson you have learned will put you in a position to find a sensible solution for all transfer pricing issues. Yes, the solution will likely not be 100% viable or "perfect," but by adhering to the basics (appropriately delineating transactions and always using the value chain analysis as a starting point and anchor), you will be in a position to at least eliminate the systemic risk => putting you at about 80% of the optimum. Dealing with the remaining 20% will require moving beyond the basics and (ultimately) some distinct experience in performing comparability analysis. Still, I decided to, at least briefly, discuss the application of the arm's length principle for two specific types of transactions: (1) management (centralized) services and (2) financial transactions. There are two obvious reasons: first, almost every MNE engages in these transactions; second, both transactions tend to be highly contentious in tax audit situations (in other words, you should have some basic strategies in your playbook).

O. Treidler, *Transfer Pricing in One Lesson*, Management for Professionals,
https://doi.org/10.1007/978-3-030-25085-0_4

The third reason (which is actually tied to the second reason stated above) for discussing management services and financial transactions is that these transactions are often perceived as being prone to be abused for tax avoidance purposes—which is why reforms/modifications for both transactions received and continue to receive a lot of attention in the context of BEPS. Throughout this book, I have tried to consistently emphasize the economic perspective on transfer pricing. An important motivation in this context was to demonstrate that the arm's length principle is (continues to be) a suitable paradigm for aligning profit allocation and taxation—even in the context of the digital economy and value chains strongly focused on IP. The key take-away for policy-makers in this context will hopefully be that future reforms (policy initiatives) should be aimed at strengthening the international consensus on the arm's length principle. The currently discussed modifications of the OECD-GL for management services and financial transactions offer ample scope for further demonstrating that the arm's length principle remains the suitable paradigm for aligning taxation with value creation.

Of course, you will be rewarded for your patience and grit by additional guidance for solving your day-to-day challenges; i.e., further complementary Excel-based TP Tools are provided for download.

4.1 Management Services

Nearly every MNE group must organize the provision of a wide range of services for its members. The assessment of these services for transfer pricing purposes is twofold. "One issue is [i] **whether intra-group services have in fact been provided**. The other issue is [ii] **what the intra-group charge for such services for tax purposes** should be in accordance with the arm's length principle." (See OECD-GL 2017a, Paragraph 7.5). Despite the ostensible simplicity of the assessment, the arm's length nature of management (and other service) fees is among the single most contentious transaction type in the context of tax audits. I have experience in tax audits where the denied deductibility of inbound service charges, even in cases that have nothing to do with intangibles or any other potentially challenging aspects, amounted to millions of Euros. And even for outbound transactions, discussions with tax auditors can be uncomfortable. I would have never believed how confrontational such a scenario could be, before being confronted with a (German) tax auditor who (rather stubbornly) insisted that the local MNE HQ provided more centralized services to foreign subsidiaries, then we charged out.

Considering that transfer (mis)pricing for services, including management services, was not identified among the main sources for BEPS (Action 11), the contentious nature of the tax audit situation described above may seem somewhat counterintuitive. To understand and appreciate the underlying reasons, I would like to advance the hypothesis that about 90% of the challenges and risks relate to issue

[i], i.e., whether intra-group services have in fact been provided, while and only 10% relate to what the intra-group charge (markup or price) should be (i.e., issue [ii]).[1]

My theory is that two mutually reinforcing phenomena are at play here.

First, taxpayers tend to be complacent when it comes to services. The root cause often appears to be that taxpayers have developed a false sense of confidence when it comes to the arm's length nature of services. In this sense, "confidence" is to be understood as trusting in one's ability (or the ability of colleagues working in the respective centralized departments) to explain to an auditor how exactly the service fees charged out are calculated. Quite often a Service Agreement will exist (at least a rudimentary one) which outlines daily rates or flat fees for some (more or less) specific services or packages of services. In respect to the applied transfer prices, taxpayers are inclined to reference "market prices"; i.e., the transfer prices are based on prices charged by independent service providers (i.e., IT consultants, management and tax consultants, accountants, etc.[2]). The issue of "comparability" and the implied requirement to adjust such market prices for all relevant differences ("quality" and, especially, "volume" are relevant here—let's not discuss the impact of adjusting for regional differences or ensuring that the sample of referenced prices can be reasonably considered to be non-biased) are often all too often neglected. When justifying the applied prices, taxpayers sometimes claim that "the prices are calibrated in way that they (over-) compensate the costs incurred for rendering respective services." Such an argument is great, and I will elaborate on this further below, but if you cannot prove that the claim is accurate, it may actually do more harm than good—and most taxpayers cannot produce sufficient proof. The cardinal sin in respect to complacency of assessing the arm's length nature of services, however, is failing to systematically be questioning whether intra-group services have in fact been provided. In quite a few cases, the tax department simply is not aware of (all) the activities rendered by centralized departments for the benefit of subsidiaries (which is bad from the outbound perspective). There are also cases, however, in which the costs accumulated on certain cost centers are allocated among all group companies, without appropriately considering whether the "alleged" services provide a benefit to the recipient (which will be highly problematic from the inbound perspective). To sum-up my rant,[3] taxpayers often have not established

---

[1]And for the 10% relating to issue ii, you can again differentiate. Discussions about a price (e.g., hourly or daily rates) of a service account for 90% of challenges and risks. In other words, only 10% relate to discussions about markups. This, in a nutshell, is why you should always strive to apply the C+ method for your services (especially when they are of supporting or low value-added nature). Stay away from (isolated) CUPs. THAT is the core recommendation that I will outline in this chapter. And, "no," there is no empirical evidence to back up this recommendation—hopefully, my reasoning will be sufficiently compelling and maybe you can put some faith in my experience.

[2]To name an example, I have seen Service Agreements (and transfer pricing documentations) referencing Big-4 fee scales as applicable reference prices.

[3]Please do not get me wrong. I know how cumbersome and frustrating it can be for the tax department to make the management aware of (and appreciate) the risks discussed above. I am

an appropriate understanding of their centralized services and lack data for corresponding documentation—the bottom line is they tend to underestimate the risks.

Second, tax auditors love to audit service fees, as most transfer pricing regulations contain rather explicit formal requirements when it comes to qualify service fees as tax deductible. Nothing is easier than assessing whether formal requirements are fulfilled and demanding adjustments in case the formal compliance is found to be a bit sketchy. Corresponding challenges are "low hanging" fruits for any tax auditor and (admittedly) a smart way to start off audit proceeding and immediately put the pressure on the taxpayer—i.e., improving the starting position of the auditor for any subsequent negotiations. Simply put, in case the taxpayer cannot conclusively demonstrate that the services have indeed been rendered, the audit will be an uphill battle. Some tax auditors tend to abuse formal rules by (more or less) blatantly refusing to assess any economic reasoning or analysis, unless the formal requirements are addressed. Core questions, which are almost always addressed, are "is there a contract?" and "can you please provide an exact account of the services rendered?[4]". Also, it should not be underestimated that many tax auditors (especially local auditors dealing with comparatively small MNEs) feel much more comfortable in assessing accounting data than with conducting an economic analysis and evaluating arm's length conditions. Nothing is easier for the auditor than to pick individual invoices from the SAP (e.g., conveniently labeled as "management fee") and inquire about the exact nature and quantity of the respective services. Being unable to provide a consistent and defensible answer will put you in an immediate disadvantage.

In respect to services, the key transfer pricing lesson is that you do not have to be very creative. In the bulk of cases, the C+ method will be applicable, and a markup can be comparatively easily derived from publicly available sources. You may quite often even be able to apply a safe harbor provision—and you should always utilize this opportunity (as outlined below). This is all well and good, but it doesn't solve much. Unless you adopt a highly systematic and transparent approach, you are prone to (sooner or later) run into the sort of difficulties outlined above. Ultimately, you will have to devote a lot of effort to identifying the services that are actually being rendered. As such, there is really no difference between an economic (businesses) and tax perspective. When writing an invoice for an arm's length transactions, you will also have to be quite specific in documenting the amount and quality of services

---

also aware that sometimes the management will (have to) refer to "strategic" or "political" reasons for justifying that (some) services are not charged to (some) subsidiaries. At a certain point, there will always be only so much you can do—but at the very least, you have to be aware of the relevant risks, as these should also be considered in the trade-off in respect to the "strategic" or "political" decisions.

[4]Many tax administrations (Romania perhaps being the most notorious case) will go so far as to demand timesheets—which in many cases would lead to an insane (disproportionate) administrative burden.

rendered. The level of detail is not the same for each client or project, but I, as a consultant, know of no client who will accept an invoice without, at least, a general description of the services and respective milestones as well as an exact account of the hours worked. The same applies when you hire a contractor to paint your flat. Depending on how complicated your arrangement will be, the contractor will provide you with a segmented account of time spend, materials used, and overheads. In such a case, it will be rather easy for you to verify whether the services have resulted in a benefit for you. There may be some case in which you are not 100% happy with the "shine" of the paint (or maybe your spouse complains that the smell of the paint makes her doubtful whether 100% organic ingredients were used as promised). Unless the contractor actually damaged your furniture, however, you will likely pay the invoice. You will also not retroactively haggle too much about the actual fee or demand proof that he indeed did spend 7 hours to paint the kitchen nook on Wednesday. The same general logic should apply for intra-group services. To determine whether a service was rendered and to develop an idea of the quality of the services, you will have to talk to the cost center and profit center managers. In talking to both transacting parties, you must determine whether the manager receiving the invoice is merely complaining about the smell of the paint or whether he has a legitimate complaint (i.e., the scope of the service was not performed as agreed, and the guest room was painted green instead of orange or—much more serious—wasn't painted at all). The level of detail of the invoice and documentation will ultimately depend on the nature of the business relationship and the ease by which to determine the benefit.

In the following, I want to outline a **systematic and transparent approach** that you can adopt for calculating arm's length fees for inter-group services. Again, I am not going to be very creative, as the following approach is closely based on the OECD-GL (2017a)[5]:

1. **Benefit Test— the Guiding Principle**: "Under the arm's length principle, the question whether an intra-group service has been rendered when an activity is performed for one or more group members by another group member should **depend on whether the activity provides a respective group member with economic or commercial value to enhance or maintain its business position**. This can be determined by considering **whether an independent enterprise in comparable circumstances would have been willing to pay for the activity** if performed for it by an independent enterprise or would have performed the activity in-house for itself." (see OECD-GL 2017a, Paragraph 7.6)
2. To start the allocation process, you will look at ALL relevant costs booked on centralized cost centers => "cost basis." Next you will eliminate all costs from the "cost basis" that do not meet the benefit test. Specifically, you will eliminate:

[5]The approach is operationalized in the **TP&C cost allocation tool available in http://extras.springer.com for download on the homepage of Transfer Pricing in Lesson.**

(a) "Shareholder activities" (OECD-GL 2017a, Paragraph 7.9–7.10): "[. . .] Such an activity would be one that a group member (usually the parent company or a regional holding company) performs solely because of its ownership interest in one or more other group members [. . .]. This type of activity would not be considered to be an intra-group service, and thus would not justify a charge to other group members. Instead, the costs associated with this type of activity should be borne and allocated at the level of the shareholder [. . .]". You should be aware that there is no universally accepted definition of shareholder activities. Generally, it seems prudent to adopt a somewhat conservative approach; with "conservative" being understood as double and triple checking whether the activities (especially those involving the top management) can appropriately be considered as a "service"—more often than not respective activities—will relate to control and monitoring functions which, from the perspective of the subsidiary, do not enhance the local business position. The OECD provides the following examples:

   (i) "costs relating to the juridical structure of the parent company itself, such as meetings of shareholders of the parent, issuing of shares in the parent company, stock exchange listing of the parent company and costs of the supervisory board". Eliminating these costs should be somewhat straightforward.
   (ii) "costs relating to reporting requirements (including financial reporting and audit) of the parent company including the consolidation of reports, costs relating to the parent company's audit of the subsidiary's accounts carried out exclusively in the interest of the parent company, and costs relating to the preparation of consolidated financial statements of the MNE (however, in practice costs incurred locally by the subsidiaries may not need to be passed on to the parent or holding company where it is disproportionately onerous to identify and isolate those costs)." The delineation of these costs may not be trivial in practice, and the fact that the OECD explicitly considers the proportionality of such an exercise is highly welcome. This provision should also provide some caution against overly simplistic approaches; i.e., even when activities are performed in centralized accounting departments which deal with foreign subsidiaries, there are good reasons to be hesitant to simply charge-out all costs only because the activities relate to foreign entities.
   (iii) "costs which are ancillary to the corporate governance of the MNE as a whole". This is pretty much the "catch-all" provision for shareholder activities.[6]

[6]The OECD also refers to further sub-categories such as "costs relating to compliance of the parent company with the relevant tax law" and "Costs of raising funds for the acquisition of its participations and costs relating to the parent company's investor relations [. . .]". Financial services will be reviewed in detail below.

(b) "Duplicative activities" shall not be charged to subsidiaries. The rationale for eliminating duplicative services is highly compelling in theory—but not always straightforward in practice. Obviously, an independent party would not procure and pay for services which are already performed in-house. The tricky question in day-to-day analysis will be to accurately delineate between different services. While many subsidiaries will have at least minimal administrative staff to deal with local issues, a substantial share of administrative activities may well be performed centrally. First and foremost, you should aim for a plausible documentation of the relevant facts, i.e., look at the organizational charts to check for inconsistencies and also cross-check the cost evolution and structure (i.e., share of cost relating to centralized services vs. local payroll and costs for local service provider or (ii) total share of overhead of total costs compared over time). If you have access to the management of the local subsidiaries, they will be the best source for identifying duplicative activities—but make sure to talk to the central departments as well. It will be fun to learn about the two, often totally different, perspectives (and it may be painful if you asked to reconcile the opposing views). But make no mistake, in many cases, these internal negotiations are exactly like arm's length transactions, e.g., solely focused on business considerations—in other words, transfer pricing at its finest (you just have to listen and take notes). Duplicative is also one of the aspects, where, based on simple economic considerations, tax authorities should adhere to a more lenient approach and refrain from demanding excessive documentations; i.e., if there were genuine duplicated services, it would be in the self-interest of the taxpayer to eliminate these "zero value-added services" as soon as possible, instead of subsidizing inefficient centralized structures. As clearly recognized in Paragraph 7.2. of the OECD-GL, "It is not in the interest of a MNE group to incur costs unnecessarily, and it is in the interest of MNE groups to provide intra-group services efficiently"—This, in my opinion, nicely sums-up the economic rationale of centralized services.

(c) "Incidental benefits": As pointed out by the OECD, "There are some cases where an intra-group service performed by a group member such as a shareholder or coordinating centre relates only to some group members but incidentally provides benefits to other group members. Examples could be analysing the question whether to reorganise the group, to acquire new members, or to terminate a division." Again, the economic logic is rather straightforward. A third party will not pay for something that it has not requested and that is not primarily or directly aimed at providing a (noticeable) benefit.[7] Sometimes, there are central divisions providing business intelligence or feasibility studies, while individual subsidiaries may ("may" as in "it appears uncertain whether benefits will be created and whether they

[7] "Noticeable" is deliberately used here, as quantifiable would arguably be a too prohibitive threshold.

would be noticeable") also participate in the benefits resulting from these activities. In such cases, the onus should be on management to substantiate the nature of the benefits. If a convincing (think internal negotiation) argument cannot be made, there is a good chance that we are talking about activities merely generating incidental benefits or plain shareholder activities.

3. Having established the appropriate cost basis for the centralized services, we can now start looking at allocating the respective costs (pricing the services). The OECD differentiates between the direct charge method and indirect charge method—and you should always look at the direct charge method first:

   (a) "*In certain cases, the arrangements made for charging for intragroup services can be readily identified. These cases are where the MNE group uses a direct-charge method, i.e. where the associated enterprises are charged for specific services. In general, the direct-charge method* ***is of great practical convenience to tax administrations*** *because it allows the service performed and the basis for the payment to be clearly identified*" (OECD-GL 2017a, Paragraph 7.21[8]). Alas, often this is not feasible. If you have an internal ticketing system or a segmented cost accounting for internal IT projects, it will often be difficult to apply direct charges to centralized services. Only in rare circumstances will you be able to apply a (reliable) CUP (remember the lesson on comparability). Often centralized services are priced by applying a daily or hourly fee—but these are almost never CUPs. Such internal prices are almost always rooted in the logic that the service provider needs to set a price which allows him to cover his costs. While it is easy to make the claim that the costs are indeed (over-)compensated, proving such claim to be correct is an entirely different matter. Ultimately, determining the costs, when talking full costs, attributable to a specific service, will require an appropriate allocation of overheads to that service—which will in turn require the use of assumptions and allocation key and which will push you to the indirect charge method. Hence, it is often an appropriate trade-off to merely identify pass-through costs (e.g., SAP license fees and other similar subscriptions) which can be directly charged to the subsidiary. The benefit for these costs can be largely taken for granted and rarely needs additional justification. Depending on the case at hand, you may want to charge a small handling fee, but generally, you can just charge such costs directly "at cost."[9]

[8]I actually always found it odd that the convenience a specific method provides to tax administrations is emphasized in such a way. But, while this certainly does not make the use of direct methods any easier, it may constitute a sort of friendly reminder that the "systematic and transparent" approach advocated in this chapter will pay dividends—i.e., knowing that you need to "sell" the use of the indirect method, you should devote at least some time to explain to the auditor why an indirect method was not feasible in the case at hand.

[9]You may want to memorize Paragraph 7.34 of the OECD-GL, "When an associated enterprise is acting only as an agent or intermediary in the provision of services, it is important in applying a cost based method that the return or markup is appropriate for the performance of an agency function

(b) While stressing the virtues of the direct method, the OCED readily acknowledges that it "can be difficult to apply in practice." The OECD outlines some sensible basic tenets that should be observed when using cost allocations and apportionment methods. The OECD states that such indirect methods are generally permissible, provided that "[a] sufficient regard [has to be been given] to the value of the services to recipients and [b] the extent to which comparable services are provided between independent enterprise" (OECD-GL 2017a, Paragraph 7.21). In respect to [a—value], the core issue is to make sure that the services shall **NOT form a main business activity** of the MNE that are provided not only to associated enterprises but also to independent parties (i.e., as in such case, it is likely that authorities would challenge that (1) a CUP can be applied and that (2) the value of the services exceeds the related costs in such a way that a mere compensation of these costs will not constitute an arm's length remuneration. In respect to [b—services provided between independent parties], we have basically already done our homework by eliminating all costs from the "cost basis" that do not meet the benefit test. The OECD (OECL-GL, Paragraph 7.24) provides two sensible examples for justifying the application of the indirect method, namely, (1) [...] "where sales promotion activities carried on centrally (e.g. at international fairs [...] or through other centralised advertising campaigns) [that] may affect the quantity of goods manufactured or sold by a number of affiliates" and (2) "[...] where a separate recording and analysis of the relevant services for each beneficiary would involve a burden of administrative work that would be disproportionately heavy in relation to the activities themselves". Especially, the second example has an immediate relevance for day-to-day transfer pricing. In general terms, it can be assumed with a reasonable degree of certainty that each MNE is intrinsically motivated to ensure a cost allocation that reflects economic reality (to facilitate an efficient allocation of internal resources). Now, when the internal cost accounting does not deem it necessary to engage in a separate recording for the costs of specific entities, then it appears quite plausible that this internal "proportionality test" should also be acceptable for tax purposes. Embedding the indirect method in a transparent process, as outlined above, and compiling the respective documentation will go a long way to generate acceptance of the approach by tax authorities. Again, the tax risks here are not minimized by creative solutions, but rather in establishing a coherent and plausible allocation process—and diligently going through the administrative motions.

rather than for the performance of the services themselves. In such a case, it may not be appropriate to determine arm's length pricing as a markup on the cost of the services but rather on the costs of the agency function itself." In other words, you generally do not charge a profit markup on SAP licenses or other pass-through items. In case the procurement and handling process are highly labor intensive, a handling-fee is appropriate. Now, if the procurement is considered a high-value-added function you need to be careful—a simple C+ method-based pricing may not be enough (especially if intangibles are involved—see below).

Thus far, we have focused on the process of cost allocations which is the most important aspect (i.e., failing to get the cost base "right" is a much larger risk than any discussion about an arm's length markup). Still, when it comes to appropriately "pricing" centralized services, the definition of "low value-added services" ("LVAS") provided by the OECD in Paragraph 7.45 of the OECD-GL (2017a) is easily the most important provision—i.e., in case the tested services qualify as LVAS, the expectations in respect to the required documentation as well as the comparability analysis for an arm's length markup are much lower compared to non-LVAS. In other words, the analysis of the economic nature of the service is equivalent (identical) to the functional and risk analysis, and you should thus devote a substantial share of your time to determine whether the tested services:

(a) *Are of a supportive nature*
(b) *Are not part of the core business of the MNE group (i.e., not creating the profit-earning activities or contributing to economically significant activities of the MNE group)*
(c) *Do not require the use of unique and valuable intangibles and do not lead to the creation of unique and valuable intangibles*
(d) *Do not involve the assumption or control of substantial or significant risk by the service provider and do not give rise to the creation of significant risk for the service provider*

In Paragraph 7.49 of the OECD-GL (2017a), you can find comprehensive list of LVAS ranging from accounting, HR, IT, to legal services. For these support services, the low value-added nature is highly intuitive. In delineating the value-added services, you should not confound the perceived "quality" of the services (i.e., the qualification of the respective employees) with the value-added contribution to the success of the MNE. In other words, only because you are looking at highly skilled (and highly paid) employees (e.g., lawyers or IT specialists), that does not disqualify these services from being categorized as LVAS. Taking the criteria (a) (supportive nature) and (b) (noncore business), it is clear that when thinking about a company such as Prima, a lawyer (irrespectively of how qualified) will not really contribute to the competitiveness of the company (i.e., sales or profitability do not correlate to his or her performance). In respect to criterions (c) (unique and valuable IP), the services listed in Paragraph 7.49 of the OECD-GL are also unlikely to be disqualified as LVAS (e.g., programming and operating an in-house CRM or SAP system is certainly commendable and an important support service to "keep the wheels spinning", but it will seldom be "unique").

While the OECD also explicitly excludes specific service categories from the simplified benefit test (see Paragraph 7.47 of the OECD-GL). This should, however, not diminish the attractiveness of the LVAS provisions for transfer pricing practitioners. The respective exclusions are mostly targeted at activities for which price setting and outcome testing will most likely be based on one of the transfer pricing methods introduced above rather than by relying on simplified benefit test anyways; i.e., we are talking about activities such as manufacturing, sales, and R&D services which are often related to the core business and commonly not perceived as centralized services anyways.[10] What is important to take to heart is that "[. . .] an activity [that] does not qualify for the simplified approach, as defined under paragraph 7.45, should not be interpreted to mean that that activity generates high returns. The activity could still add low value [. . .]" (See OECD-GL 2017a, Paragraph 7.48). In day-to-day practice, you would generally apply the same process for all low value-added centralized services, irrespective of whether they are included in the OECD positive or negative list (i.e., obviously the restrictions to manufacturing, sales, or financial services.)

The OECD stresses three main advantages of the simplified benefit test or simplified approach, specifically (Paragraph 7.52 of the OECD-GL 2017a):

1. Reducing the compliance effort of meeting the benefits test and in demonstrating arm's length charges
2. Providing greater certainty for MNE groups that the price charged for the qualifying activities will be accepted by the tax administrations that have adopted the simplified approach when the conditions of the simplified approach [. . .] have been met
3. Providing tax administrations with targeted documentation enabling efficient review of compliance risks [. . .]

The absolute "clincher" (bar none) in this context is the stipulation contained in OECD-GL Paragraph 7.54: "[. . .] because of the nature of the low value-adding intra-group services discussed in this section, such determinations [substantiate the willingness of a recipient to pay for services] may be difficult or may require greater effort than the amount of the charge warrants. **Tax administrations should therefore generally refrain from reviewing or challenging the benefits test when the simplified approach has been applied** under the conditions and circumstances discussed in this section." In other words, the OECD explicitly recognizes that in case a transparent process is applied for allocating costs incurred from rendering routine services, there is very little risk that any tax avoidance effects will be a result from such everyday business practices. This exact type of regulation we as transfer pricing practitioners should embrace. We are certainly capable of conclusively demonstrating whether a service has a low value-added nature and we are also capable of going through the motions of a standardized allocation procedure. If the "reward" for the respective efforts is that the tax authorities will refrain from opportunistic challenges, I would suggest that that is certainly a worthwhile tradeoff.

[10]Other excluded activities relate to financial transactions (which will be reviewed below in the next chapter), extraction, exploration, and processing of natural resources as well as insurance and reinsurance (which are rather idiosyncratic transactions anyways). The only odd choice of the OECD was to include purchasing (of materials used in manufacturing) on this negative list—in many business models, purchasing activities are of supporting nature and are not linked to unique and valuable contributions to the total value-added. The trickiest exclusion on the OECD list are the services rendered by "senior management" ("other than management supervision of services that qualify as low value-adding intra-group services under the definition of paragraph 7.45"). I am not saying that

Following the process outlined above, we will ensure appropriate determination of the cost pool (Section D.2.2. of Chapter VII of the OECD-GL 2017a) as well as the allocation of low value-added services (Section D.2.3. of Chapter VII of the OECD-GL 2017a). In respect to the applicable markup, Paragraph 7.61 of the OECD-GL (2017a) offers a highly welcome "safe harbor" by clarifying that "The same mark-up shall be utilised for all low value-adding services irrespective of the categories of services. The **mark-up shall be equal to 5% of the relevant cost** [. . .]. The mark-up under the simplified approach **does not need to be justified by a benchmarking study.**" That provision is one of the most sensible provisions contained in the OECD-GL, as it aligns the economic rationale of profit allocation (arm's length remuneration for a routine service) with the principle of proportionality (why benchmark for a remuneration on routine, low value-added services, when you know that 5% fall within any type of conceivable inter-quartile range).[11] The bottom line is it eliminates a completely unnecessary source of uncertainty and field of (unrewarding) discussion with tax auditors.[12] The OECD limits the scope for applying the safe harbor be stating that "[. . .] low value-adding intra-group services mark-up should not, without further justification and analysis, be used as benchmark for the determination of the arm's length price for services not within the definition of low value-adding intra-group services, nor for similar services not within the elective, simplified scheme." The takeaway here is that based on a thorough classification of the services, it will generally be feasible to justify a consistent application of the low value-added markup for a low value-added services. The documentation and reporting requirements for the simplified approach outline in Paragraph 7.64 of the OECD-GL (2017a) also is sensible, namely, (1) clarify low value-added nature of the services, (2) draw up a contract, and (3) documenting the calculations of the allocations (cost pool and allocation keys). It would simply be negligent not to adhere to these basic requirements.

Let's summarize the systematic and transparent approach for calculating inter-group services in the form of our familiar "**decision tree for inter-group services**"[13]:

[11] As empirical underpinning of this assessment, you can (among others) refer to EUJTPF (2009)—yes, the study is 10 years old, but the core insight (the median of various service categories remaining close to 5% irrespective of economic cycles) can be considered stable.

[12] Policy-makers and tax authorities should not only agree on this point but also actively pursue to extend the scope for applying this safe harbor—what needs to be realized here is that, provided the classification of the services as "low value-added" is accurate, there should be virtually no discussion about tax avoidance—the service provider receives an arm's length remuneration. End of story. Thus, any restrictions or limitations, such as those outlined in Paragraph 7.63 of the OECD-GL, should be used sparingly.

[13] Again, the approach is operationalized in the **TP&C cost allocation tool provided in http://extras.springer.com for download**.

1. Does a specific activity provide a respective group member with economic or commercial value?
   (a) If "no" => well, you are not looking at an activity that is to be remunerated as a service, i.e., you are not even looking at an intercompany transaction. As the reason for this conclusion will most likely be rooted in the nature of the business relationship between the related parties (including their functional profiles), you may want to check that your presentation of the business provides sufficient clarity. For transfer pricing documentation purposes, you can even think about explicitly stating that the local entities are acting largely autonomously in respect to the relevant activities (if this is deemed likely to help avoiding any misunderstandings on the part of the authorities)
   (b) If "yes," you have to establish the appropriate cost base by eliminating all costs from the relevant cost centers which do not meet the "benefit test" (shareholder activities, etc.) and subsequently proceed with the allocation process
2. Is the application of the direct method feasible?
   (a) If "yes" => Draft a respective contract and calculate an appropriate price. The application of a direct method will either require availability of segmented data (see above). For all costs that cannot be allocated based on the direct charge method, you will have to proceed with 2(b)
   (b) If "no" => The indirect method, as outlined above, will be applied. You will have to determine a transparent allocation mechanism which ensures that the costs (remaining after progressing through steps 1b and 2a) to be charged to each recipient are proportional to the respective benefit provided by the service. For most services, the identification of appropriate allocation keys will be rather straight forward (e.g., the number of users for IT services, number of employees for accounting or payroll services). In some case, you will also have to be a bit more creative (most in-house departments will, however, will have established sensible allocation keys that can also be applied for tax purposes). Yes, one could arguably write a PhD thesis on cost allocation, maybe even an intriguing one, but in day-to-day practice, you will generally be able to cope with identifying suitable allocation key.
3. Do the services qualify as low value-added services?
   (a) If "yes" => be happy and apply the simplified benefit test or simplified approach (see above)
   (b) If "no" => double-check the provision contained in OECD-GL (2017a), Paragraph 7.48. If the service is (1) not related to the core business of the MNE (2) does clearly not involve any intangibles, you can factually also apply the simplified approach in such a case—how else would you proceed? Two aspects would merit some additional consideration though—(1) you will have likely be well advised to compile some additional documentation (i.e., the "further justification and analysis" mentioned by the OECD) and (2) you

should think about alternatives to the safe harbor provision of the 5% markup. Maybe you will have to get creative here too and some idiosyncratic services (e.g., insurance and reinsurance or the exploitation of natural resources) will indeed demand an in-depth analysis. For most MNEs, having progressed through the earlier steps, there generally will not remain many services (costs) to be allocated. When you find this assumption to be true, you should invoke the stance of the OECD in respect to the principle of "proportionality" and treat the remaining services (arguably including those rendered by "top and middle management") analogous to the services for which you have applied (and documented) the simplified approach (in such a case, you should, however, pay particular attention to the next step).

4. Remember IP

   This is really the ultimate "sanity check at that stage." I did think (quite hard) about whether to discuss intangibles at an "earlier" point in this chapter—and more prominently. I trust, however, that anyone reaching this stage in the book sufficiently appreciates that intangibles merit special attention and will not be let astray to adopt a default cost plus 5% type of remuneration when trying to identify an arm's length transfer price for the utilization of unique and valuable intangibles. Hence, I decided it is much more important to emphasize the benefits of adhering to a standardized and transparent process.

   Also, from an economic perspective, the relevant assumption here is straightforward. Namely, that support processes will not be based on utilizing unique and valuable intangibles, as either (1) the respective processes are not really of supportive nature or (2) the respective intangibles are not truly unique and valuable. Companies utilize their unique and valuable intangibles to earn money, not to render centralized support services. Hence, when you really believe that your tested activity (service) is based on unique and valuable intangibles, there are good chances that the guidance on centralized services is not the one you seek—this also applies in case you are looking at a case were multiple members of an MNE collaborate in creating and exploiting an intangible. In such a case, you should revisit the section on PSM and take another look at the DEMPE concept (see above), but please stay clear of mingling the utilization or exploitation of IP with the provisions for centralized services.

It would certainly be feasible to discuss centralized services in more detail (e.g., individual allocation keys), but the added depth of discussion would not contribute to minimizing systemic tax risk in proportion to the effort required to understand and apply the more nuanced lessons. Adhering to the basic insights, i.e., (1) identify the benefit related to an activity and (2) establish a transparent process to "filter" the applicable cost base, is certainly the best strategy for everyone being tasked with reviewing the transfer pricing system for centralized services within any MNE—the "bigger" ones may want to add a little more depth or detail to their analysis, but the basic approach will always be the same.

4.2 Financial Transactions

Just as nearly every MNE must organize the provision of a wide range of services for its members, it must also ensure that all members have access to sufficient financial capital.[14] While short-term funding (liquidity) is often ensured by integrating all subsidiaries in the cash pool of an MNE, medium- and long-term financial needs are usually met by extending intercompany loans. Ostensibly, financial transaction may not appear particularly fascinating from a transfer pricing perspective. After all, comparable data (interest rates) appears to be readily available—either external data from the financial markets (e.g., from providers such as Bloomberg) or based on internal data (e.g., agreements with local banks). It is true that applying a CUP can often be feasible for financial transactions. Applying the CUP for financial transactions, however, may not be quite as straightforward as someone (including your CFO) may be inclined to think. The core insight for avoiding pitfalls in relation to financial transactions is to closely observe one of the basic lessons outlined above—i.e., **ensuring an adequate delineation of the transaction.** While the OECD-GL (2017a) are largely silent on how to apply the arm's length principle to financial transactions, the ongoing BEPS consultation procedure provides sensible insights—which shall be reviewed in detail below (first for loans and subsequently for cash pooling).[15]

Loans

In a nutshell, the discussion process illustrates that the OECD feels that tax avoidance structures are not primarily based on MNEs exploiting the (inevitable) bandwidths for setting arm's length range but rather on implementing financial structures that a misaligned with the economic circumstances or substance of a business relationship.[16] In other words, the OECD and national tax authorities display a clear commitment to review and challenge the arm's length nature of financial transactions that are geared to shift profits from companies operating in

---

[14]While I will not talk (immediately) about "financial services," many financial transactions between MNEs are fundamentally of "supportive" nature and may thus be viewed as "services." We shall discuss below that this does have implications for the choice of an appropriate transfer pricing method—as was discussed multiple times, a cost-oriented pricing may likely be appropriate for services.

[15]Specifically, we will review the discussion contained in OECD (2017b). To be sure, the Discussion Draft does not reflect an "international consensus," but I find that the issues discussed therein are of utmost relevance for taxpayers and offer sufficiently specific ideas (guidance) to appropriately address core issues such as the selection of an appropriate transfer pricing method.

[16]That position is certainly shared by many national tax authorities, and you will find a plethora of national tax cases dealing with (re-classifications) of financial transactions (some will be mentioned below).

high-tax jurisdictions to financial holding located low-tax jurisdiction. When charging interest rates of 10% and above (in 2019) to your subsidiaries, you will have to prepare a (more or less) ironclad CUP that appropriately accounts for the specific circumstances of the business relationship. Tax authorities are not only likely to critically assess whether your CUP (benchmark) satisfies the relevant comparability requirements but will also question whether it is appropriate to apply a CUP in the first place (or whether third parties would have applied a "cost of funds" approach in comparable circumstances). As we have already learned, such a re-classification constitutes a "systemic risk" and translates to substantial tax risks.

Just how serious the OECD is in delineating financial transactions is reflected in the complex and comprehensive economically relevant characteristics and indicators the OECD considers to be useful for determining arm's length interest rates, namely, "[...] *the presence or absence of a fixed repayment date; the obligation to pay interests; the right to enforce payment of principal and interest;* ***the status of the funder in comparison to regular corporate creditors***[17]*; the existence of financial covenants and security; the source of interest payments; the ability of the recipient of the funds to obtain loans from unrelated lending institutions; the extent to which the advance is used to acquire capital assets* [...]" (see Paragraph 16 of the Discussion Draft on Financial Transactions).

The core aspect of the discussion is arguably to be seen in the (largely new) emphasis on adopting a two-sided perspective when evaluating the arm's length nature of a financial transaction. The OECD emphasizes that, "Independent enterprises, when considering whether to enter into a particular financial transaction, will consider all other options realistically available to them, and will only enter into the transaction if they see no alternative that offers a clearly more attractive opportunity to meet their commercial objectives. In considering the options realistically available, the perspective of each of the parties to the transaction must be considered" (see Paragraph 19 of the Discussion Draft). While the lender should consider the cost of funding as well as other investment opportunities, the borrower would consider the amount of funding necessary to meet its operational requirements as well as its ability to service the debt.

There is certainly merit to the economic rationale outlined by the OECD. A two-sided perspective will, however, render the application of a (stand-alone) CUP to be (much) more challenging and will thus require MNEs to modify previously adopted best practices.[18] These (old) best practices where mostly focused on assessing the creditworthiness of the borrower and identifying market interest rates

[17]I highlighted this characteristic, because I hold the opinion that the "two-sided" perspective on the transaction has the most substantial impact on the arm's length or comparability (as discussed below).

[18]How much trickier the pending modifications of the OECD-GL will render the application of the CUP for financial transaction will remain to be seen. Looking at Paragraph 20 of the Discussion Draft, one may get the impression that finding a sufficiently viable CUP will be (close to) impossible. Specifically, the OECD emphasized that the required adjustments for a CUP will most likely be feasible for quantitative factors (such as currencies of a loan), whereas adjustments

No	Type	Description	Borrowers Location	Borrower S&P Rating	Maturity	Base Rate	Margin
1	Credit, Loan, Revolving Credit, Revolving Loan	A Holding company (industry: media and entertainment) entered into USD 75 million credit agreement with one lender. The proceeds will be used for working capital needs	Bermuda	B+	2023 (unspecified)	Prime Rate[a], +0.5%	9.5
2	Credit, Loan	Borrowers (industry: vacation ownership management) entered into a USD 27.5 million secured loan agreement with a financial institution	US	B+	2023	Libor	3.25
3	Credit, Loan, Term Loan senior	Manufacturer (industry: vacation ownership management) entered into a USD 100 million senior term loan agreement with one lender. The proceeds will be used for working capital and general corporate purposes	US	B, negative	2018 (projected)	Prime Rate	8.25
4	Credit, Loan, Revolving Credit, Revolving Loan	A Holding company (industry: media and entertainment) entered into USD 75 million credit agreement with one lender. The proceeds will be used for working capital needs	Bermuda	B+	2023 (unspecified)	Prime Rate, +0.5%	9.5

Fig. 4.1 Exemplary Database Search for comparable loans. [a]Federal Funds Effective Rate (source: own illustration (based on database output))

charged to independent borrowers with a similar credit rating—thus, essentially reflected a one-sided perspective or analysis. Unsurprisingly, most aggressive tax schemes involving interest payments were based on determining a weak (non-investment grade) stand-alone credit rating for the borrowing entity. The comparability analysis in turn was heavily (myopically) focused on sifting through financial data (including loan databases[19]) to identify interest rates charged to borrowers with a similar credit rating.

The results of a database search for a USD loan may look something like those illustrated in Fig. 4.1 (note: the search strategy was based on the following rather

for qualitative factors (e.g., business strategies), which could be attributed to a substantial impact in the context of a two-sided perspective, are expected to be much more difficult.

[19]As a side note, I want to clarify that I will be discussing loan benchmarking only on an "exemplary" basis in this chapter. Yes, there are multiple commercial databases available for identifying individual loans (and yes, I am a subscriber as well). Based on my experience with these databases, however, I am convinced that you will rarely be able to identify loans that are sufficiently comparable to your tested transactions. Now, I was never really satisfied with the results derived from such benchmarks since about 2008—and I would suggest that the databases have not (dramatically) improved since then (most offer surprisingly limited data and continue to have a rather pronounced bias for US data). With the stance of the OECD and national tax authorities becoming even more strict in regard to comparability requirements, the attractiveness of utilizing databases is certainly not enhanced. While identifying individual loans may (theoretically) constitute the "cleanest" CUP, I find that relying on aggregated data (i.e., data on bond spreads and credit default swaps) provides for a much more robust and reliable comparability analysis. Obviously, these are just my private sentiments—and I will have to compile the relevant empirical underpinning at some point in time—I would only advise at this point that you treat very carefully when encountering (the idea of) benchmarking loans by utilizing commercial databases.

broad criteria: "Loans" granted in 2018, in USD, with amounts up to 100 Mio, Borrower to be located in North America or Europe with a rating of B+ or lower[20]):

The dilemma should be obvious. You will often deal with a limited number of potential comparables (note loans No. 1 and No. 4 are identical, and thus, one should be deleted to avoid redundancy). While the example may not be entirely representative, it is indeed often uncertain whether you will find a loan that constitutes a reasonable match for your tested transactions—especially when applying the strict comparability criteria that are the hallmark of a CUP.

Looking at the results shown in Fig. 4.1, loan No. 2 immediately stands out as differing from the other potential comparables (i.e., in terms of (1) being secured and (2) the lender being a financial institution). So, it can be firmly ruled out that loan No. 2 will be in the same group of comparables as loans No. 1 and 3 => this is a clear "either or case,", i.e., claiming that you have identified a range between 3.25% and 9.5% would make little economic sense (even pre-BEPS). Now, the main parameters pf loans 1 and 3 seem to reflect a reasonable comparable; i.e., in a real-life case, you would (have to) download the loan agreements from the database at this point to verify that the parameters are indeed comparable (i.e., verify the description and check for covenants)[21]. Assuming you could (somehow) verify that the difference in maturity between the loans has no material impact on the comparability (or you can perform a reasonable adjustment[22]), the analysis would result in an arm's length range between about 9% and 10%. Well, considering the economic situation on the financial markets, 10% is certainly a steep price for procuring funds, but for borrowers with a low credit rating (no securities), applying such rates for an inter-company loan should not automatically reflect non-arm's length pricing. In real life, you should, however, anticipate that the tax auditor in the jurisdiction of the borrower will show some interest in your benchmark. And, how confident would you feel with such results?

[20]The following table contains the results I obtained from the database (slightly abbreviated in respect to the displayed criteria—however, only four potentially comparable loans were identified (really three as No. 1 and No. 4 are actually the same loan), indicating that data on loans is not as abundant as data for companies/margins). I refrained from utilizing the screenshot to avoid any publications and rights issues.

[21]This process is the equivalent to the manual screening when applying the TNMM and needs to be documented diligently when you want to have a tax viable loan benchmark (I did not engage in this fun exercise here)—and in most cases, it is quite as relevant as when screening comparable companies in TNMM benchmarks, simply because there is limit to the amount of parameters you can reasonable assess for a loan and the database providers (mostly) do a credible job when integrating the loans into the database. Essentially the loan database contains a pre-screening (which is not the case for company databases) and your primary task is to (1) verify that the information and (2) (more challenging) interpret the results.

[22]Ceteris Paribus one would assume that the lower interest rate for loan 3 is due to the shorter (lower) maturity/duration)—the qualifications of "projected" and "unspecified" contained in the database would obviously necessitate a closer analysis.

Well it really depends to a substantial degree (almost exclusively[23]) on how you derived the rating of B+ or lower for your borrower. A tax auditor successfully challenging your rating (i.e., claiming a rating between A+ to A– reflects the creditworthiness of your borrowing entity more accurately) would, keeping all other search criteria unchanged, obtain drastically different end results. Not only would the number of potential comparables increase to 27 (giving the auditor more flexibility in defining sensible comparability and exclusion criteria), but the resulting arm's length range would most likely not be higher than 1.5–3.5%. In other words, you are looking at a total difference of about 7.5%, which translates in substantial transfer pricing risk. So, in case your rating is not (close) to ironclad (i.e., matching the quality of an actual rating assigned by rating agency), you will have to stomach quite a substantial degree of uncertainty in respect to the tax viability of your benchmark.

To give you some perspective of what level "ironclad" implies in this context, I want to elaborate a little. The OECD states, in somewhat lukewarm terms, that "[. . .] credit ratings **can serve** as a **useful measure** of creditworthiness and so **help to identify** potential comparables" (see Paragraph 58 of the Discussion Draft) and that "[. . .] Information is readily available in many **lending markets on the different rates of interest charged for differently rated enterprises** and such information may usefully **contribute to benchmarking studies** for interest rates charged by associated enterprises" *(see Paragraph 61 of the Discussion Draft)*. Both statements are interesting in respect to the fact that they are phrased rather carefully and that they refer to (the general effects of) ratings that can be observed on the financial markets (especially the wording of Paragraph 61 seems to suggest a distinctly aggregated view on the data). While the OECD also recognizes that commercial tools available to calculate a rating (i.e., I presume the OECD refers to "Moody's RiskCalc" product) may generally be useful for benchmarking purposes (see Paragraph 63), the outright attack on such tools follows in Paragraph 64: "The credit rating methodology used in commercial tools **differs significantly from the credit rating methodologies applied by independent credit rating agencies** to determine official credit ratings. For instance, such tools generally use only a **limited sample of quantitative data** to determine a credit rating. Official credit ratings published by independent credit rating agencies are derived as a result of **far more rigorous analysis** which includes quantitative analysis of historic and forecast company performance as well as detailed qualitative analysis of, for instances, management's ability to manage the company, industry specific features and the company's market share in its industry."

Naturally, you are free to disagree with the OECD on this issue—I certainly do. To me, it seems rather evident that the OECD adopts a romanticized view on the rating methodology applied by rating agencies. Academically, it would be quite an

[23]Of course, the other parameters will also matter, but not nearly to the same extent—this is also why the benchmarking (manual screening) for loans is not quite as existing (relevant) for loan benchmarks as it is for TNMM.

intriguing question to analyze the extent (maybe quantified by notches) by which the results obtained from commercial tools differ from those of the rating agencies. I am perfectly willing to concede that there will likely be a (statistically significant) difference and that the "quality" (i.e., accuracy in predicting default) or the agencies ratings will be superior (although I would not bet on the statistical significance). I am, however, not quite sure that we would be asking the correct question; i.e., do the differences really matter for transfer pricing purposes? As discussed in the opening chapters, there is no one "correct" price (especially when introducing qualitative parameters) and we can absolutely stomach some fuzziness (e.g., 2–3 notches) without having any qualms about whether or not the arm's length principle can be reliably applied for financial transactions. While the transparency of the commercial tools may be limited, tax auditors are certainly in a position to perform plausibility checks (i.e., the usually have ready access to the same tools) so that any angst of BEPS-related effects seems blown out of proportion (especially when considering the second aspect—and when talking about the principle of proportionality with a straight face[24]).

Now, on top of the uncertainty about the viability of internal ratings, the OECD's advocacy of a two-sided perspective has the following implications:

First, you MUST address the question whether utilizing the stand-alone rating is appropriate. Based on the emphasis that the OECD is attributing to account for "group effects" or "incidental benefits," there can be little doubt that the viability of a stand-alone rating will be rather low (even IF the quality is deemed acceptable).[25] The question is certainly not trivial and poses no small challenge from a transfer pricing perspective.

Economically, I see no reason to question the basic rationale adopted by the OECD. Yes, independent companies (i.e., those companies not being part of a MNE) will negotiate directly with a lender (a financial institution of their choice), who will base his calculation of the applicable interest rate on the stand-alone rating of that

[24]Seriously, especially when looking at SMEs and non-blue chip companies of this world, how much of a burden of proof do you want to place on a taxpayer? Utilizing a commercial tool to determine a credit rating for the purpose of applying interest rates that are commensurate with the arm's length principle reflects, if anything, a serious effort to be compliant. A tax administration challenging this approach should at the very least bear the burden of proof that the rating applied by the taxpayer is implausible. The last thing we need is to introduce "rebuttable presumption" (see below) that the taxpayer has to cope with. We need to consider that comparable data for financial transactions is, compared to other kinds of intercompany transactions, readily available for tax authorities to conduct plausibility checks. Hence, it only seems reasonable to leave to burden of proof with the tax authorities. If this means that a more thorough analysis is requited on the part of the tax authorities, I can see no harm in this—as, even based on OECD guidance, tax authorities should conduct risk-based tax audits (i.e., focus their resources on cases that merit a closer analysis instead of second-guessing some degree of fuzziness resulting from the use of commercial rating tools.

[25]To be fair, the OECD is not necessarily to be viewed as the champion for advocating the focus on group benefits when pricing financial transactions—there is an ever-increasing number of national court cases illustrating that tax authorities are also supporting this view (especially in high-tax jurisdictions).

Group Status	Definition	Rating
Core	Entities that shape the identity of the MNE and are integral to the future strategy of the group. There is a high likelihood that the rest of the group will support these core entities [i.e. HQ and entities contributing unique and valuable intangibles]	Group Rating ("GR")
Highly strategic	Entities that are "close" to being integral to the future strategy of the group. While not quite as essential as core entities, these entities would likely be supported by the rest of the group	GR *minus* one notch
Strategically important	Less integral to the group compared to highly strategic entities. The rest of the group would, however, be likely willing to provide additional liquidity or capital.	Generally, three notches above SAR[a]
Moderately strategic	Even less integral to the group than the strategically important entities. While there is still potential for some support from the group, it would most likely be limited	Generally, one notch above SAR
Non-Strategic	Entities with no strategic importance to the group; i.e. entities that could be sold in the near to medium term (or substituted by procuring services from third parties)	Stand-Alone Rating ("SAR")

Fig. 4.2 Exemplary down-notching process. [a]The alternative approach here (see footnote 27) would be to just continue the down-notching by applying GCR *minus* two or three notches. This will ensure appropriate differentiation to highly strategic entities while also mitigating the problem that you do not (want to) have a SAR available for each entity. When moving on to moderately and non-strategic entities, you would down-notch even further (i.e. minus four to five notches) (source: own creation (based on Standard & Poors))

company (as there obviously is no group rating to consider). This will, however, not imply that any subsidiary must be priced based on the stand-alone rating, as the lender will consider all relevant facts and circumstances of a transaction—and these include group effects. The OECD outlines the basic rationale as follows: "In determining the likelihood of support from other group members in the event of the borrower getting into financial difficulty, the relative status of an entity within the group may help determine what impact if any that potential group support has on the credit rating of a debt issuer. Typically group members are considered to be more, or less, likely to receive group support according to the relative importance of the entity to the group [. . .]".[26]

A best practices approach for operationalizing this rationale is the so-called down-notching process. Starting from the rating for the headquarters or "core" entities of the group, the creditworthiness of whom is reflected in the group rating, each group member will be assigned a credit rating that reflects is strategic importance relative to the core entities; i.e., the less strategically important, the smaller will be the implied incidental benefits. Figure 4.2 illustrates a variant of the down-notching process as applied by rating agencies (e.g., Standard & Poors)[27]:

---

[26]Paragraph 69 of the OECD BEPS Public Discussion Draft on Financial Transaction

[27]See Standard & Poor (2013). Note: For practical transfer pricing purposes, the approach proposed by S&P is not 100% ideal, as it features the stand-alone credit profile (SACP) of the noncore entities. The entire point of using a down-notching procedure is (in line with the principle of

Second, you need to consider "the lender's perspective in the decision of whether to make a loan, how much to lend, and on what terms, will involve evaluation of various factors relating to the borrower, wider economic factors affecting both the borrower and the lender, and other options realistically available to the lender for the use of the funds" (see Paragraph 49 of the OECD Discussion Draft). From a borrower perspective, the decision to procure funding will also depend on the purpose of utilizing the funds in the context of the business strategy. Specifically, when a loan is extended by the parent entity to a routine entity (contract manufacturer or low-risk distributor), it needs to be considered that the borrower will only earn a routine remuneration that cannot be cannibalized by interest payments. Considering that in such a case the principal (lender) has an immediate interest in the borrower business activities (i.e., earning the residual profits), it would reflect arm's length behavior to calculate the interest rate based on the cost of funding incurred rather than on financial market data (i.e., applying the C+ method rather than the CUP).

Cash Pooling

Cash Pooling arrangements are also increasing scrutinized by tax authorities. In the context of BEPS, one of the core concerns of tax authorities in relation to cash pooling is that a cash pool leader (located in a tax friendly jurisdiction) is often allocated all synergy gains resulting from the pool arrangement. The OECD Discussion Draft (Paragraph 111) outlines a highly restrictive and one-sided presumption; namely, that "In general, a cash pool leader performs no more than a co-ordination or agency function with the master account being a centralised point for a series of book entries to meet the pre-determined target balances for the pool members. Given such a low level of functionality, the cash pool leader's remuneration as a service provider will generally be similarly limited."

The presumption of the OECD is clearly to be interpreted in the anti-tax avoidance context of BEPS. And again, the basic rationale makes economic sense. Independent parties certainly are assumed to negotiate to split the synergy gains resulting from pooling resources that reflect their respective contribution to the creation of the synergies.[28] In this context, it is thus intuitive that cash pool

proportionality), however, to determine a reliable credit rating for entities for which you do not have a rating. A more pragmatic approach, which will generally result in credit rating with a similar degree of reliability with those of the S&P, is to apply the down-notching (i.e., GCR minus "a couple of" notches) for all entities, not merely entities qualified as "highly strategic" => as illustrated in the figure.

[28]To be sure, independent parties will generally not enter a cash pooling arrangement, but I do not see why the separate entity approach (fiction) applied to MNEs would limit the appropriate applicability of the arm's length principle to a transaction such as a cash pool. Many critics of the arm's length principle claim that this fiction of separate entities is at the root is the main conceptual weakness of the arm's length principle, as MNEs will engage in transactions that independent entities will not. While the application of the arm's length principle in such cases is certainly more challenging, it is the flexibility inherent in the arm's length principle and the close link to bargaining theory which enables the taxpayers (and the tax authorities) to approximate (validate) allocations of

participants would be willing to forfeit all synergy to a cash pool leader who only provides administrative services without having "skin in the game." What needs to be pointed out (especially vis-à-vis the tax authorities) is that most cash pool structures are based entirely on commercial reasons, such as maximizing the return on liquidity for the group as a whole and minimizing the cost of funding as well as reducing transaction costs of moving money between bank accounts, while any tax motivation is absent.

To accurately determine (1) the synergies resulting from the cash pool arrangement and to (2) determine an arm's length allocation of the benefits among the participants is extremely complex. Also, even if you apply highly sophisticated mathematical allocation mechanisms, you will generally not be immune to challenges on the underlying premises applied in your calculations. This sub-chapter is thus aimed to help you navigate through the most vital questions of cash pool transactions and to ascertain a sufficiently comfortable tax position without having to invest a disproportionate administrative effort. As will be illustrated below, the best way to communicate the absence of a tax motivated cash pooling arrangement and (ultimately) to defend the arm's length nature of the applied interest rate is to **avoid "extreme" allocations** (of synergies) and to be aware of a (limited) number of red-flag issues.

The most pragmatic "official" guidance (currently) known to me is not provided by the OECD but rather by the HMRC ("International Manual", INTM500000).[29] The following example, based on the HMRC International manual, nicely illustrates how to identify (avoid) extreme allocations:

Figure 4.3 summarizes the position (local cash balances) of the example MNE without a cash pool arrangement in place—incurring total (net) interest payments to local banks of 8000:

In this simple example, entering into a cash pooling arrangement thus results in a net benefit of 8000, i.e., equivalent to the saving of external interest payable.[30] These benefits (of 8000) need to be allocated among the participants according to the arm's length principle.

Now, the example MNE establishes the cash pool arrangement shown in Fig. 4.4. The entity based in the Netherlands is assuming the function of cash pool leader. The

the synergies among MNE entities that conceivable reflect an outcome to be expected in negotiations between independent entities in comparable situations.

[29]To be sure, however, according to my interpretation, the HMRC position is consistent with the OECD discussion reviewed above—the International Manual on Cash Pooling dates from April 2016 (updated 2018).

[30]The pooling of the cash on one master account could naturally (but does not always) result in the MNE being able to obtain more favorable deposit rates. The respective benefits would also have to be added to the total net realized benefit (see Fig. 4.4).

	External Borrowing rate	External Deposit rate	
	2.50%	0.50%	
jurisdiction	funding required	excess funds held	interest payable
UK	−100,000		−2500
Germany	−300,000		−7500
Luxembourg		400,000	2000
Netherlands			
	−400,000	**400,000**	**−8000**

Fig. 4.3 Exemplary cash pool (source: own illustration (based on HMRC example))

	External Borrowing rate	External Deposit rate		INTERNAL Borrowing rate	INTERNAL Deposit rate	
	2.50%	0.50%		0.50%	0.50%	
jurisdiction	funding required	excess funds held	interest payable	INTERNAL interest payable	INTERNAL interest receivable	**Delta (Benefit)**
UK	−100,000		−2500	−500		2000
Germany	−300,000		−7500	−1500		6000
Luxembourg		400,000	2000		2000	0
Netherlands						
	−400,000	**400,000**	**−8000**			8000

Fig. 4.4 Cash pool—non-arm's length structure (source: own illustration (based on HMRC example))

external interest rates are held constant. The internal Deposit rate was set equal to the external Deposit rate, while the internal Borrowing rate was set substantially lower than the external Borrowing rate:

Figure 4.4 illustrates that based on the adopted price setting, all benefits are allocated to the entities located in Germany and the UK which are in a borrowing position. The tax authorities in the Netherlands and Luxembourg would conceivably challenge the arm's length nature of the extreme allocation.

Clearly, the example MNE would realize quickly that the initial price setting was not optimal (not only from transfer pricing perspective) and aim to calibrate the interest rates in a way that leads to a more "balanced" allocation, i.e., raising the internal borrowing rate to 1.25% and the internal deposit rate to 1.00%. Figure 4.5 illustrates the resulting profit allocation among the pool participants:

Figure 4.5 illustrates that the resulting allocation is a more balanced, with each participant sharing in the benefits. Now, whether the allocation is in "exact" proportion to the contributions of the parties can admittedly be subject to (much) debate; i.e. should Luxembourg not be entitled to a larger share of the benefits, as it is the

	External Borrowing rate	External Deposit rate		INTERNAL Borrowing rate	INTERNAL Deposit rate	
	2.50%	0.50%		1.25%	1.00%	
jurisdiction	funding required	excess funds held	interest payable	INTERNAL interest payable	INTERNAL interest receivable	Delta (Benefit)
UK	−100,000		−2500	−1250		1250
Germany	−300,000		−7500	−3750		3750
Luxembourg		400,000	2000		4000	2000
Netherlands						
	−400,000	**400,000**	**−8000**			7000

Difference of 1000 is the benefit allocated to the cash pool leader.

Fig. 4.5 Refined cash pool structure (source: own illustration (based on HMRC example))

company contributing the excess funding, which makes the cash pooling feasible? You could make a variety of arguments, but you would also have to realize that in real life the balances of the participants can be quite volatile (i.e., Luxembourg could well be in a borrowing position in a future period) and that the calibration of the interest rates and argument for an arm's length allocation would have to appropriately account for the "dynamic" nature of the pool. The bottom line should be, as formulated by the OECD (Paragraph 102 of the Discussion Draft), that "No member of the pooling arrangement would expect to participate in the transaction if it made them any worse off than their next best option." Aiming at a balanced allocation (a sort of middle-ground) when calibrating the internal interest rates will thus often be a sensible starting point or default position.[31]

When the cash pool leader (as presumed by the OECD) is indeed merely providing a service function, calibrating the interest rates has a sort of anchor; i.e., the residual benefits (i.e., in the aforementioned example 1000) allocated to the cash pool leader (i.e., in the above example in the Netherlands) should be calibrated to cover the cost of the cash pool leader for providing the services (i.e., assuming that the cash pool leader in the above example incurs costs of 950, this would imply a remuneration of cost-plus 5% and likely reflect arm's length conditions).

Aside from ensuring a balanced allocation of the benefits, the following potential "red flag" issues should also be considered when setting-up a cash pool and can serve as a sort of implementation guideline:

(a) Most third-party banks would have limits on overdraft facilities => *you may want to stipulate sensible threshold that reflects the operational liquidity requirements of the participants.*

[31] In case the cash pool leader may have a non-investment grade credit rating, this could justify allocating a higher share of the benefits to the depositors as a compensation for the increased risk. While there is no clear rule in this respect, it may be prudent when calibration the interest rates to, when in doubt, give a slight preference to the depositors.

(b) There should be clearly defined criteria (thresholds) to determine when a balance goes from being "short term"—repayable on demand and charged short-term borrowing rates—to "long term," where at arm's length the debt would likely have been restructured into a loan on a long-term rate => *As a rule of thumb balances that are consistently in a credit or debit position for a period of > 12 (maybe 24) months should be analyzed. In case it is determined that there is no compelling business rationale to keep the (complete) cash balance in the cash pool, it should be transformed into a loan.*

(c) If large balances are being held on overnight deposit, it would be expected to explain the commercial reasons for holding the money on a short-term basis => this essentially combines (a) and (b).

(d) From an economic and administrative perspective, there is generally quite a high degree of flexibility when setting up a cash pool arrangement—provided that the issues highlighted above are appropriately addressed, the arrangement (profit allocation) should be commensurate with the arm's length principle (why would you put administrative shackles on such an internal arrangement?[32]).

To be sure, this chapter can only serve as a basic survival guide. The excel tool referenced in Annex F will support you in calibrating the interest rates for your cash pool—taking into account multiple periods.

[32]While you should approach the cash pooling with a "positive" attitude and tailor the administrative processes according to your preferences, you should also accept that a contract will ensure consistency and transparency (which is always helpful when entering a tax audit—see below).

Chapter 5
Documentation and Tax Audits

In this final part of the book, I want to provide some general remarks in respect to preparing a transfer pricing documentation and to slugging-through a tax audit. Both subjects, especially tax audit proceeding, exhibit a myriad of local (national) particularities[1]—hence, making "general" comments is not entirely trivial and I do not want to dwell on different formal requirements, but rather outline thoughts that are immediately relevant for implementing The Lesson of this little book.

I have referred to specific aspects relating to transfer pricing documentation roughly 30 times throughout the preceding chapters. While these frequent (inescapable) references already provide an indication of the importance of having an appropriate (consistent!) documentation available, I want to emphasize the following "soft factors" that may help you in making day-to-day decisions when being (t)asked to actually compile (or update) the transfer pricing documentation[2]:

1. *Do not be discouraged and ask questions* => being assigned with compiling the transfer pricing documentation is never a thankless task. You are bound to learn a lot about the inner workings and strategic orientation of the (your) company and interact with management personnel from various departments. You will find yourself in a situation in which you are expected and allowed to ask questions—and sometimes to challenge the status quo. Asking questions is the core to applying The Lesson. You really need to understand the perspective of the

[1] In respect to the tax audits, one could argue that you would even have to account for "regional" differences, as, speaking from a German perspective, the "flavor" of audits in Bavaria can be quite distinct from those in Berlin—and I am sure similar statements could be made in other countries as well.

[2] Please understand that the following list is non-exclusive and reflects a distinctly personal view—depending on who you ask, they may well emphasize different aspects, and you will have to understand and embrace that ultimately you will need to find your own approach; i.e., while a consultant can explain the legal requirements of a documentation and also give you a broad indication of the required scope, you need to take ownership and feel comfortable in knowing that a one-size-fits all solution does not exist.

O. Treidler, *Transfer Pricing in One Lesson*, Management for Professionals,
https://doi.org/10.1007/978-3-030-25085-0_5

decision-makers (managers of the profit or cost centers) and can ask them straight-up whether specific prices are "negotiated" vis-à-vis other MNE entities or (if not) what the underlying rationale of the applied transfer prices is from a business perspective.

2. *Understand the essential nature of the business model* (see Chap. 2.1) => The objective of asking your questions will always be to develop a sound understanding of the business model of the MNE. The challenge is to not get caught-up too early in individual transactions but to contextualize these transactions with a clear and focused "big picture" of the business. The key challenge is to develop such a "picture" and to construct a consistent "storyline,"; i.e., you need to identify the "character" of the MNE in the sense that you understand the core value drivers and the USP—which also implies to identify those functions or processes that are of supportive (low-value added) nature. As a transfer pricing consultant, this task is one of the most "fun" elements of your job; you will get to know a lot of different business models—and, based on this experience, you can always bring some broader "perspective" to the table, which can have a tremendous value in a documentation process (i.e., as an "outsider," it is sometimes easier to establish an adequate scope and avoid being suffocated by (from a tax and transfer pricing perspective) comparatively minor issues).
3. *Be concise and establish an adequate level of segmentation* (see Chap. 2.1) => Having developed a sound understanding of the business model will enable you to apply the lesson on appropriate delineating (aggregating) transactions. Once you have outlined your storyline, every effort should be made to "stay on point." As a general rule, you should avoid overloading your documentation with information that is not immediately relevant to "getting your story across" (to the auditor—see next point). Ensuring a concise presentation will demand a lot of discipline, and it will only be feasible when you have truly gained a thorough understanding of your business model. There are two immediate benefits to a concise presentation: (a) too much information will dilute your storyline, confuse the tax auditor, and (on balance) result in more questions and a more tedious audit[3], and (b) your life will be easier and your will spare administrative resources.[4]

---

[3]Sometimes you will come across a notion (often made by tax consultants or CEOs not being familiar with even the basics of transfer pricing) that is somewhere along the lines of "oh, we will just pour so much information over the auditor that he doesn't know where to look and will be discouraged—facilitating a beneficial audit outcome." Be careful not to buy into this line of thinking. It might have been a viable strategy in the early 2000s, but tax auditors are generally getting up to speed and have learned were to look—especially in a post-BEPS context, the data (transparency) available will render such a strategy futile and will generally put you in an uncomfortable position—i.e., you put yourself at risk to have to backtrack or defend parts of the documentation that was contained in the "data dump," and this is inconsistent with your storyline. So, if you have nothing to hide, there is rarely any advantage in engaging in such shenanigans.

[4]The rationale is simple, the more concise your documentation, the less time you need to spend writing (and updating) it. It can also be very efficient to define thresholds for which transaction categories will be documented in detail—additional information can then be made available to the

4. *Have a clear purpose* => The ultimate purpose for compiling a transfer pricing documentation *must* always be understood as being prepared for the next tax audit. Documentation is first and foremost about compliance. That statement is in no way meant to belittle the importance of a documentation. On the contrary, considering that tax authorities introduce an ever-stricter regulatory framework (including penalties), ensuring compliance is vital. You want to put yourself in a good starting position for the tax audit (see below), and an appropriate documentation is, perhaps, the single most important "homework-type" of assignment you need to address. In many jurisdictions (i.e., Germany) having an appropriate documentation will ensure that the burden of proof will fall on the tax authorities (at least nominally)—and this is why you cannot afford to neglect your homework. To be clear, you do not need to provide the authorities with a "perfect" all-comprehensive-type of documentation—as emphasized above a concise presentation of the storyline is what ultimately matters.[5] The bottom line is that you want to tell "your story" to the auditor in the most convincing (and pleasant) way possible—this does include utilizing language he can understand.

Similar to sports, being prepared is everything. Establishing a transfer pricing system which is based on the tenets outlined in this book and having prepared an appropriate documentation is as good a preparation as you can have.[6]

---

authorities upon request. Naturally, many software solutions have been introduced to the market during the last couple of years (including some good ones from independent providers, i.e., systems not "tied" to Big 4 consulting). For many MNEs, adopting digital solution will make a lot of sense—it is just a question of a cost-benefit analysis (at least up to this point). The bottom line is that you want to invest your transfer pricing budget in ensuring a tax viable transfer pricing structure not in writing reports.

[5]After all, the documentation is merely a starting point. It should be consistent and accurate, but you can always cover some of the "finer points" in course of the tax audit (i.e., "on request"). In other words, while you should not engage in shenanigans (see above footnote), you do not need to expect a "pad on the back" from the auditor for going the extra mile (i.e. documenting an individual transaction type with a volume of <20 k€ when your total cross-border transaction volume exceeds 20 Mio. €)—that is just no sensible proportion and you should utilize thresholds. In some (mostly smaller jurisdictions in Eastern Europe), the use of such thresholds is discouraged and sometimes you will have to yield to these local requirements—in general terms, I think such rules reflect poor policy-making and border on harassment. This is really an issue the business community should speak-out on more courageously. In the context provided by this book, it should be clear that such initiatives are not designed to pave the way for avoidance structures or to limit transparency but rather to make policymakers aware that observing the principle of proportionality will not hurt them (there is no real risk in a tax gap resulting from these minuscule transactions) while at the same time keeping the administrative burden for taxpayers within reasonable limits (see also my words to tax auditors).

[6]For the sake of completeness, it needs to be pointed out that MNEs do have to opportunity to enter into so-called "advanced pricing agreements" (APAs) (or tax rulings). These instruments can be sensible in the case of highly complex or unorthodox transactions, i.e., when you are uncertain how tax authorities are going to react to your transfer pricing structure. Proactively disclosing these structures to the authorities has the benefit to eliminate the uncertainly for future audits (if you have multilateral agreements), as you can obtain a sort of "pre-approval." In terms of the administrative burden, the APAs are, however, far from enticing. They are time-consuming and will cost a lot of

As, nonchalantly, stated by the OECD (Paragraph 4.2 of OECD-GL): "It is possible that taxpayers and tax administrations may reach differing determinations of the arm's length conditions for the controlled transactions under examination given the complexity of some transfer pricing issues and the difficulties in interpreting and evaluating the circumstances of individual cases."

This statement is accurate and should not be surprising. It should also not facilitate any doubts about the practical applicability of the arm's length principle. Tax authorities should naturally be free to audit the transfer pricing systems and to critically examine the compliance with the arm's length principle. The previous chapters have highlighted several red flags a taxpayer should be aware of and it was evident that even though a taxpayer may devote a lot of earnest effort to observe the arm's length principle, some room for discussion and interpretation in respect to the arm's length nature of specific prices and margins may remain.

In day-to-day practice it is, however, important how the audit procedures are interpreted by individual tax authorities (auditors). One lamentable development is that (somewhat coinciding with BEPS), tax auditors increasingly seem to enter transfer pricing audits with a deeply ingrained distrust, which often translates in excessive demands for supporting information and heavy reliance on testing formalistic issues—in sum, taxpayers are often confronted with a disproportionate administrative burden. Here, it would be welcome to if more emphasis would put on limiting audits to cases in which there is a clear infringement of the arm's length principle. The core issue in this context is the principle of proportionality—and taxpayers should not hesitate to invoke it as much as possible. It is always recommended to enter the audit with an adequate (documentation) and to communicate the transfer pricing system in a proactive manner. Respective behavior should ideally dispel (most of) the distrust an auditor may harbor.

One effective proactive approach, when possible, is to utilize the kick-off meeting to the audit for giving the auditor a brief (Power Point) presentation of the transfer pricing documentation, before handing over the actual document. The additional preparation required for such a presentation is minimal, e.g., you essentially prepare 6–8 slides with a diagram of the main transactions, the functional and risk analysis, as well as the chosen transfer pricing method and the results of the comparability analysis. Such a presentation will contribute to have a sensible "focus" for the tax audit and help to avoid the necessity of answering written inquiries and procuring documents for transactions that are clearly of subordinated nature. Having established a transfer pricing system that is based on the tenets outline in this book, you have really nothing to hide, and the advantages of such a proactive

money—in respect to documentation requirements, there is also no real benefit in applying for an APA proceeding (it should also be pointed out that any application can naturally be rejected). While APA are frequently discussed in transfer pricing publications, only few (large) MNEs systematically utilize APAs (involving less than 4% of the more than 11,000 MNEs with the USA) for most SME APAs can safely remain irrelevant. For a detailed account of APAs, including current statistics and policy considerations, I warmly recommend the article by Eden and Byrnes (2018).

approach will most often outweigh any potential drawbacks (additional costs or stirring the interest of the auditor).

Now, this is where the guidance ends for now. The bottom line is, having worked through "Transfer Pricing in One Lesson", you should no longer be scared of the next tax audit.

Chapter 6
Closing Remarks: A Kind Word to Tax Auditors and Policymakers

Throughout this book, the tax authorities might at times have been characterized as a sort of "opponent" of taxpayers. To be sure, there is a competitive element involved in almost every tax audit, i.e. when stepping on to the bazaar, everyone is trying to secure a favorable bargain. It should be clear, however, that all respective comments were intended to be understood in the spirit of good sportsmanship.

What is important to recognize is that tax auditors are bound to follow (enforce) the regulations issued by their respective national tax authority. Some of these national regulations may offer more leeway to the individual auditor than others, but no auditor will be able to escape the regulatory framework. While transfer pricing audits will thus remain a "people's business" (i.e., the individuals participating in the bazaar will have a substantial influence on the outcome), the quality of audit outcomes (in the sense of finding agreement on the arm's length nature of transfer prices) always depends on the quality of the regulatory framework. Overall, the BEPS project constituted a comprehensive and wide-ranging reform package that seems suitable to limit the extent of aggressive tax-avoidance schemes. Specifically, the enhanced focus on economic substance, i.e., giving precedence to the functional and risk analysis over legal ownership of intangibles or contractual allocations of risks, is a sensible reform and may hopefully evolve into evolutionary approach to modernizing the arm's length principle. In this context, it is to be hoped that the regulatory frameworks will also put stronger emphasis on the economics of transfer pricing that also allow (force) the auditors to apply the arm's length principle in a sensible manner (i.e., not hiding behind overly formalistic regulations).

Keeping in mind that the empirical evidence of the extent of profit shifting can be considered as weak (preliminary), policymakers may be well advised to adopt a comparatively passive approach, i.e., refraining from introducing further or additional anti-avoidance provisions and wait for the effects of the BEPS project to

O. Treidler, *Transfer Pricing in One Lesson*, Management for Professionals,
https://doi.org/10.1007/978-3-030-25085-0_6

"materialize." Idiosyncratic national anti-avoidance regulations[1] will exacerbate the uncertainty that is faced by taxpayers. Regulators could also help by keeping politization of transfer pricing contained; i.e., if the public position reflects the narrative that most MNEs exploit the arm's length principle, it is hardly surprising that tax audits are increasingly characterized by a climate of distrust with many auditors adopting an aggressive stance. One of the most important regulatory aspects for the day-to-day practice would be that national tax authorities re-think their internal allocation of resources. Currently, there seems to be an undue focus on SMEs, whereas stricter audits of large MNEs would seem much more sensible (efficient) from an administrative perspective, including introducing more generous thresholds for small companies (i.e., exempting them from formal requirements to compile a full-scope transfer pricing documentation[2]).

Alas, I fear that the development is going into a different direction. The most worrisome development in 2018/2019 is arguably to be seen in the discussion on the tax challenges of the digital economy. After individual member States have started to introduce a national tax on digital economy, the European Commission, issued a policy proposal in the summer of 2018 to "reform corporate tax rules." The intention of this proposal is to enable Member States to tax profits that are (allegedly) generated in their territory, even if a company does not have a physical presence there—based on a so-called "digital presence" or "virtual permanent establishment," which is deemed to exist when certain criteria (turnover or "user"-based thresholds) are exceeded. These policies reflect that financial ministries and tax authorities in Europe are no longer primarily concerned with minimizing aggressive tax structures by modifying existing principles and regulations but are rather looking for ways to generate additional revenues by implementing entirely new taxation schemes (often relying of formulary apportionment approaches)—which threatens to systematically erode the consensus on the arm's length principles.[3] The OECD has initiated a large-scale public discussion in the beginning of 2019, in which several options were introduced for tackling the perceived challenges of the digital economy. Unfortunately, the OECD proposals did not reflect a firm commitment to the arm's length principle. Instead, the OECD seems willing to allow for elements of formal apportionment when dealing with marketing intangibles. The positive aspect in this context is that the transfer pricing community was very active in engaging in the

[1]Note: Some of the worse effects are related to excessive regulation regarding formalistic requirements, i.e., an ever-increasing scope of required documentations (including detailed data on *ex ante* financial data such as forecasts and budgets).

[2]In Germany, for example, this threshold is stipulated at 600,000 € (cumulative volume) for service transactions and 6,000,000 € for all other transactions. Even start-up companies quickly exceed these thresholds and frequently have to cope with suffocating audit procedures—a more lenient regulation would greatly help these smaller companies to get off the ground without any material danger of trigger tax gap effects. Naturally, this would apply not only to transfer pricing but in tax in more general.

[3]For detailed comments, see Treidler (2019).

public discussion procedure and voice comparatively harsh criticism against the OECD proposal.[4]

Without addressing these issues further at this point, it should be evident that discussions about the arm's length principle will be with us for years to come. I hope this book, elaborating on the basics of transfer pricing and the practical application of the arm's length principle, can make a small contribution to this discussion. Ultimately, I can think of no better promotion of the arm's length standard than entrepreneurs embracing the concept and emphasizing (and also demonstrating) that it indeed ensures a sensible alignment between the economic realities of their business and taxation.

[4]Whereas the OECD previously compiled all public responses in one or two PDFs, it actually had to set up a "drop box" to publish all the comments received regarding the digital taxation. For all practitioners and students interested in international regulation of taxation, these responses are a treasure trove of information. I also contributed my two cents, specifically emphasizing that the proposals of the OECD (i.e., by adopting a default position of allocating (allegedly high-value) market intangibles to local sales entities) erode the established consensus that a low-risk distributor is conceptually not entitled to a share in the residual profit. While some of the more intricate points of the public discussion are beyond the scope of issues discussed in this book, you will find that the current discussions actually touch heavily upon the basic arm's length principles we discussed in this book.

Annexes

Annex A. Questionnaire: Transfer Pricing Basics

The following questions are designed to provide a starting-point for compiling a transfer pricing documentation. At this stage bullet-point answers and ballpark estimates are sufficient. Your answers will enable us to develop a basic understanding of your business as well as to identify potential transfer pricing related risks. We would utilize the information in our preparations for a workshop or kick-off meeting, during which we conduct an in-depth interview on the topics touched upon below.

Identification of Relevant Facts and Circumstances

1. What are the key characteristics of your industry (competitive landscape, overall profitability, main factors for pricing, importance of IP) and what is your unique selling proposition?
2. What kind of cross-border relationships/transactions among related entities are most relevant within your group?
3. What is the hierarchical relationship between the group companies, i.e. is your group characterized by a centralized or decentralized organizational structure? Which entities determine (negotiate) prices with end customers?
4. Can you quantify the volume of intragroup transactions (overall and in respect to different kinds of transactions)?
5. Please describe the pricing mechanism utilized in intragroup transactions, i.e. which transfer pricing methods are applied (cost plus, resale minus, etc.)?
6. Has the pricing mechanism been subject to changes/modifications within the last 5 years?

O. Treidler, *Transfer Pricing in One Lesson*, Management for Professionals,
https://doi.org/10.1007/978-3-030-25085-0

7. Have assets, particularly intangibles, or individual functions (production, sales) been transferred between related entities, i.e. in the context of business restructurings?
8. Have some entities incured (continuous) losses? Please indicate the underlying reasons?
9. Which intangibles are crucial for the success of your business? Which entity has developed the intangibles? Does this entity still have ownership?
10. Did any transfer pricing related issues surface during earlier tax audits?

Annex B. Checklist for Benchmark Studies

Guidance for Integrating Benchmark Studies into the Local File

One of the core tasks in compiling the Local File is integrating one or, in case the local entities participate in different categories of intercompany transactions, multiple comparability studies into the documentation. Considering that the quality of benchmark studies prepared by local advisers tends to be highly heterogeneous, it is important to **ensure that all studies comply with the quality standards stipulated by the MNE headquarter** (exemplary standards are outlined below). To facilitate an efficient and consistent documentation process the following steps are to be followed in sequential order (for each transaction—note: While the arm's length principle is to be applied on a transaction-by-transaction basis, transactions that are "closely related" may be evaluated jointly (OECD-GL, paragraphs 3.9–3.12)—the level of aggregation (identification of **transaction categories**) is the prerogative of the headquarter):

Note: This guidance solely refers to benchmark studies comparing the (net) profit indicator of the tested party to a range of comparable companies. For guidance on benchmark studies for license rates (royalties) or interest rates (loans, cash pooling), please refer to separate guidance.

- Utilize **pan-regional benchmark studies** (i.e. pan-European or pan-Asia)—if available.

Headquarter (or regional management) will provide benchmark studies for all (major) transaction categories within the group, i.e. contract manufacturing, low risk distribution or intercompany loans. In case the regional entity participates in a respective transaction, either as tested-party or as the principal (entrepreneur), it is compulsory to utilize the benchmark studies provided by headquarter or regional management.

Task 1 => ***check*** if studies are available for the transaction categories in which your entity participates

If a pan-regional study is available proceed with Task 2—if no study is available proceed to guidance on "commissioning a local benchmark analysis"

Task 2 => **upload** (integrate) study to Local File. Verify whether the margin of the tested party falls within the arm's length range identified in the benchmark. In case the margin fallswithin the range, no further action is required (proceed to Task 3). In case the margin falls outside of the identified range, please "flag" the transaction as "identified risk"

Task 3 => When (if) the local file is ***submitted*** to a local tax advisor for high-level review, it needs to be emphasized that all benchmark studies are subject to the quality standards of the group. In reviewing the benchmark, the advisor must be instructed to focus on answering the following question: "Will the local authorities accept the pan-regional comparables identified within the benchmark study?"

While pan-regional studies are in general widely accepted—and supported by international organizations (OECD and EU), some tax authorities exhibit a strong preference for local comparables. By default, local advisors tend to advocate performing a local benchmark. Due to the limited availability of potential comparables at national level, however, it is seldom that such a study will produce more reliable results—especially when the country in which the tested party is located was integrated in the geographical scope of the search strategy.

In case the review of the local auditor does not raise "red flags", no local benchmark must be commissioned, and the submission can be flagged as "finalized". In case of red flags, please proceed to Task 4. The following would qualify as red flags:

- The benchmark is "certain" to be discarded by local authorities => the advisor must cite specific references to the applicable local regulations and explain why a benchmark that is commensurate with the OECD approach will not be considered as adequate by local authorities. => More specifically, it must be answered why the guidance contained in paragraph 3.35 of the OECD-GL are deemed not to be applicable.
- The local advisor identifies severe methodological or technical deficiencies and inconsistencies in the submitted benchmark => any such reports must be forwarded to headquarters.
- The local advisor can credibly demonstrate that a local benchmark would most likely result in a "substantially" different arm's length range—with "substantially" being defined as the margin of the tested party falling outside of new/adjusted range => One relevant issue to consider in this respect is comparability adjustments for so-called "location specific adjustments" => local advisor should address paragraphs 1.142 and 1.143 as well as (more generally) 1.144ff. of the OECD Guidelines (2017a).

Task 4 => Request proposal for a local benchmark (based on the guidance for "commissioning a local benchmark analysis"—see below) as well as a proposal for alternative solutions, i.e. secondary or alternative method (see OECD-GL 3.58).

Commissioning a Local Benchmark Analysis

The quality of benchmark studies is rather heterogeneous. Combined with a rather critical stance on the application of the TNMM (i.e. by German tax authorities), benchmark studies are prone to be challenged during a tax audit—sometime only for 'tactical purposes'. Especially in case of rather "exotic margins" (i.e. OM (FCMU) $<3\%$ for a domestic tested party or OM (FCMU) $>8\%$ for foreign tested parties, tax authorities show a propensity to challenge benchmark studies. In order to avoid/ minimize respective challenges the following (minimal) standards must be observed when commissioning a local benchmark analysis:

- Study must be based on database that are widely accepted (utilized) by tax authorities, i.e. Amadeus or Orbis by BvD. Databases merely containing "large/ listed" companies (i.e. Capital IQ) are not acceptable, as the potential comparables are likely to exhibit a non-routine functional profile as well as "independency issues".
- Technical data (search file/"srh") are to be submitted by the provider. The study must be 're-produceable'. Failure to document the technical data will result in "formal" (hard to refute) challenges by tax authorities.
- Manual screening procedure => the scope (# of potential comparables) as well as the parameters considered in setting-up the analysis are the key-determinants of the "quality of a benchmark". To an adequate level of comparability, it is essential that the analyst manually reviews the information for potential comparables available on the respective homepages. A screening that is limited to reviewing the data/information contained in the database will not yield accurate results (in some countries such a 'pure database screening' is explicitly considered to be inadequate and will result in the rejection of the analysis). The following rules of thumb are to be understood as "minimum quality standards":

  - At least 120 potential comparables to be included in manual screening
  - The "final set" should include between 10 and 20 comparables
  - Homogenous composition of final set must be targeted and should be validated
  - No "excessive range" => i.e. an IQR ranging from 1 to 15% is highly "suspect"—indicator of insufficient homogeneity => actual range must be "tailored" results of tested parties
  - The search strategy should consider company size vis-a-vis the tested party— as a general rule, large companies (>50 Mio. € in revenues) tend to exhibit non-routine functional profiles—and should be scrutinized accordingly
  - It should be checked whether the final set contains local comparables. Not only for "cosmetic" purposes, but rather as a "hygiene factor". It should further be checked whether local comparables exhibit a systematic bias (i.e. are margins either below or above IQR). In case no local comparables are included in the final set, the local file must make reference to the OECD guideline or local regulations in order to justify the use of pan-regional studies

If the quality of the analysis is found to be "questionable", please carefully evaluate the tradeoff of utilizing the benchmark vs. the use of alternatives. You should be aware—guard against—the tax authorities engaging in cherry-picking based on your benchmark—i.e. please check how sensitive your result is in case one or two comparables are challenged.

Annex C. Application of a CUP License Fee: Case Study Variation for Prima Asia

A CUP will always be difficult and would be discouraged in the context of the Prima Asia case study. Should Prima Asia, however, have a higher degree of autonomy compared to case study discussed above, a CUP (license benchmark) could be utilized to determine an arm's length royalty/license fee.

Based on the relevant facts and circumstances the following search criteria could be utilized[1]:

- *License Date: Starting 1.1.2016* => when applying a CUP for intangibles (brands) you generally should be mindful to limit the timeframe of the search, as "older" IP is unlikely to be comparable (effects of timing in the context of a CUP have been discussed above)
- *License Type: Exclude: Technology, Software; Manufacturing* => You can select (and exclude) the type of IP/ Agreement that you are looking for. As prima Asia utilizes the marketing intangibles of Prima, it was deemed appropriate to exclude non-sales related agreements
- *NACE 2.0 Code: 46.43; 46.5 and 47.4* => the selected NACE codes should ensure that the license agreements relate to the "consumers electronics industry" that is relevant for Prima. Similar to benchmarking for comparable companies it is generally sensible to avoid being too resistive at this stage—as you will have to verify the comparability of individual license agreements in the context of the manual review anyway, you should be more lenient in the beginning to identify a sufficient sample of comparable license agreements. You can also apply key-word to fine-tune your search but considering that the database (no matter which commercial database you will utilize) inevitably contains much fewer license agreements compared to a TNMM benchmark, such a fine-tuning will often not be relevant.
- *Regional Scope: Asia* => As the license extended to Prima Asia is limited to the Asian Market, it is sensible (required) to limit the search accordingly—A caveat in applying CUPs for licenses is that most commercial databases contain

[1]The following example is based on search in an actual commercial database. I have, however, modified all names as well as some of the qualitative output to avoid copyright issues => the quantitative information, however, was left unchanged.

Description of Agreement	Geographic Scope	Base	Royalty Rate
1) License to maintain an operate the "Ong Bak 9000", massively multiplayer online role-playing game in Thai language and to grant users access to this version...	Thailand	Gross Sale	20%
2) License under trademarks and brands "I know this camera" and "I know this camera & pixel designs" to use with the products; i.e. consumer televisions and computer monitors	India, Nepal, Bangladesh	Avg. Sales Price	2%
3) License under licensors trademark related to large-scale, multi-color, real-time digital displays and LED lighting	Unspecified / global	Total Revenue	3%
4) License to use licensors brand "Unknown Master" to manufacture, distribute and sell LED TVs, LED monitors etc.	Unspecified / India	Total Turnover	1%
5) License to use "Melrose 90210" trademarks in dishwashers, gas stoves, water dispensers, water heaters (gas or electric) – [note: related party agreement]	Unspecified / China	Net Sales revenues	0.3%
6) License to use "Huge Pelican" trademark and picture the refrigerators and freezers - [note: related party agreement]	Unspecified / China	Net Sales revenues	0.3%
7) License under licensor's patents to technology, which aims at improving the efficiency of central air conditioning....	Global	Sale	5%
8) License to use "Pure Gold" trademark and picture in production, sales and ad campaign of washing machines - [note: related party agreement]	Unspecified / China	Net Sales revenues	0.3
9) License under patent rights to develop, make use, sell and import products in the field of power and load monitoring of industrial equipment... [note: one party is an NGO]	Global	Net Sale	2% - 4%
10) License under patent rights to make use, sell and import "touch sensors" comprising fine lines of copper metal.	Global	Net Sale	4%

Fig. C.1 Exemplary results of a license database search (source: own creation—based on output of commercial database)

abundant agreements for the USA, but contain only a comparatively small amount of agreements related to other regions

– *License Base: Sales* => You can choose the basis on which the licensee fee is calculated (profits, costs, assets, others). In the case of Prima Asia, a license rate based on sales (revenues) appears to be most appropriate.

Figure C.1 summarizes the results obtained from the above search strategy.

What can we conclude here? First, despite the rather lenient search strategy the number of potentially comparable agreements is rather limited. Second, even based on the rather short description it is feasible to exclude the majority of license agreements [all except: Agreements (2), (3) and (4)] as being not sufficiently comparable to a license arrangement between prima and Prima Asia.[2] Third, at least three agreements fulfill the "ballpark" criteria for utilizing a CUP for prima

[2]The Agreements (5) (6) and (8) are obvious (compulsory) exclusions due to the fact that they relate to (like the same!) intercompany agreement. Agreement (9) is also be excluded as neither the IP seems comparable and one party is a NGO (which, in my view, isn't an automatic exclusion but

Asia. Forth, the qualitative analysis required will be extensive. While having only three potentially comparable agreements does not render the attempt to apply the CUP to be futile, a diligent analysis of each license agreement would be required to ascertain whether the degree of comparability will be adequate. Having a limited number of comparables will, however, preclude the use of statistical tools (e.g. calculating an interquartile range) to enhance the reliability of the results. The fact that the range of royalties applied within the potentially comparable agreements is quite narrow (1–3%)[3] would, however, be rather positive in the case at hand.

While you may sometimes be able to identify a larger number of potentially comparable agreements (especially for the US), the above example is quite representative of the results you will be confronted with. While the 1–3% would provide a sensible indication of an arm's length range, the tax viability will generally be low when relying on a stand-alone CUP. In other words, you should always aim to validate your CUP but applying the PSM (or at least a rule of thumb analysis—see below).

Rules of thumb, such as the "Goldscheider Rule", could provide an additional option in case you prefer (for whatever reason) to structure the transaction as a license arrangement rather than an RPM based system.[4] While the use of rules of thumb have been explicitly discouraged by the OECD-GL (see Paragraph 2.10 and Paragraph 6.144), these rules, because they quickly deliver results, unsurprisingly remain popular with many practitioners. Such rules essentially provide a sensible starting-point for a hypothetical negotiation process that is derived from the so-called "classical 25% rule".[5] While often mis-understood as a simple shortcut to determine royalty rates, the rule, when properly understood, provides a comprehensive (multiple-step) analytical framework that is based on an empiric evaluation of

which would demand additional scrutiny). Agreements (1), (7) and (10) are also obvious exclusions, as they relate to IP that is substantially different from the IP utilized by Prima Asia.

[3]Note: It is note quite clear how the "base "avg sales price" would be "translated to "net sales"—i.e. here an analysis of the Agreement will be required. If it is feasible to calculate a corresponding net sales rate, the agreement could still be utilized as a comparable.

[4]Note: The following is not to be mis-interpreted as advertising the widespread use of a rule of thumb. Please, also do not confuse the application of such a rule with the PSM—the results; i.e. a license rate determined by utilizing a rule of thumb by conducting a hypothetical negotiation process will not be equivalent with the result from applying the PSM—most of all because the "profits to be split" are not equivalent; i.e. as explained in the previous footnote the "profits to be split" would be based on "combined profits" (i.e. also considering the costs incurred at the level of Prima), whereas the rules of thumb would only consider the profits realized by Prima Asia (which will be much more straightforward and always enable you to derive a respective royalty rate—hence the appeal of the rules of thumb).

[5]This methodological approach is also known as the "Goldscheider Rule", which is (roughly) similar to the so-called "Knoppe-Formel" that is frequently used in Germany as a pragmatic approach to gain a rough indication for the arm's length nature of royalty rates—see also Vögele et al. (2015).

significant private transactions.[6] The basic rationale of the classical 25% rule is "*dividing revenues in a hypothetical negotiation* [with] *a dividing ratio is tentatively chosen at the outset of the hypothetical negotiation—one that is possibly, but not necessarily, equal to 25:75, depending on the prior experience of the parties or their initial impressions at the outset of the exercise*". The baseline values for the dividing ratio of 25% [to the Licensor] and 75% [to the Licensee] are based on empirical results. Considering that the empirical results exhibit a certain degree of variance, it seems sensible, as proposed by the Knoppe-Formula, to apply a baseline range between 25–33% [to the Licensor] and 66–75% [to the Licensee].

Having established a baseline value, it is essential to conduct a qualitative analysis of the value of the intangibles in order to assess whether (relative to the baseline) a higher or lower dividing ratio will reflect arm's length conditions—the relevant analytical framework can be summarized as follows, "what is the 'Next Best Alternative' to Licensing Available to the Licensee"? Specifically, the maximum royalty that would normally be acceptable to a Licensee is one that is equal to the cost of the next best available alternative. These alternatives are principally[7]:

- Use of the technology at the risk of a lawsuit
- Independent development of the same or similar technology
- Design of the licensee's operations around licensor's property rights;
- Licensing of comparable property rights from another source
- Avoidance of any use of technology within the purview of the licensor's property rights

Additional relevant questions are:

- Is the quality of the invention, as patented, such that it is technically very difficult or economically very expensive for a third party to design around, or otherwise avoid?
- Are purchasers of the product or users of the process of which the patented invention forms a part, aware of the presence of the impact of the invention, and is this awareness crucial to the decision to purchase or use?

Looking at the intangibles contributed by Prima it appears evident that, prima Asia does not have any realistically available alternatives to procure similar

[6]See Goldscheider (2011). In this article, Goldscheider specifically emphasizes that the 25% rule is not to be applied as a rule of thumb, but rather only as a baseline value, which subsequently as to adjusted to the characteristic economic circumstances of a specific transactions (i.e. analysis of available best alternatives as well as the value- added functions of the parties). As such, Goldscheider appropriately addresses the criticism that is often directed against the lack of reliability of oversimplified rule of thumb solutions. (again, also compare Vögele et al. (2015), Chapter O, RN 627ff).

[7]Compare Goldscheider (2011). In this context, Goldscheider specifically refers to 'Georgia-Pacific' decision as well as to the "The Book of Wisdom" concept, which was first cited by Judge Howard Markey, the first Chief Judge of the Court of Appeals for the Federal Circuit, in his Fromson opinion.

intangibles from different providers at lower rates. It is further evident that prima Asia neither has the financial capabilities or the technical knowhow to develop a similar technology. Moreover, as highlighted in the context of the functional and risk analysis there is no question that the quality of the inventions and developments contributed by Prima constitute the main value driver. It also should be considered that Prima continuously undertakes substantial investments to further improve the software (i.e. accumulating knowhow and enhancing the value of the intangible). Cumulatively, the qualitative analysis provides a strong and reliable indication that the baseline dividing ratio would have to be adjusted to the benefit of Prima to reflect an arm's length result, i.e. reflecting the upper-end of the baseline range or even slightly exceeding that range.

Considering the above, an appropriate arm's length royalty rate can reasonably be expected to reflect a dividing ratio between 30–40% [to Prima] and 60–70% [to Prima Asia].

Bibliography

Baumgartner, B. (2018). Value creation analysis for transfer pricing purposes. *International Transfer Pricing Journal, 25*(2), 2.

Brem, M., & Tucha, T. (2013). *Kennzahlen Verrechnungspreismanagement.*

Eden, L., & Byrnes, W. (2018). Transfer pricing and state aid: the unintended consequences of advance pricing agreements. *Transnational Corporations, 25*(2), 9–36.

European Joint Transfer Pricing Forum (EUJTPF). (2009). *BM contribution to illustrate available generic evidence relating to intra group services profit margins*. DOC: JTPF/018/BACK/2009/EN.

European Joint Transfer Pricing Forum (EUJTPF). (2013, November). *Report on compensating adjustments*. DOC: JTPF/009/FINAL/2013/EN.

European Joint Transfer Pricing Forum (EUJTPF). (2018, October 24). The application of the profit split method within the EU. In *Working paper discussed at the EUJTPF meeting*. DOC: JTPF/012/2018/EN.

European Joint Transfer Pricing Forum (EUJTPF). (2019, March). *The application of the profit split method within the EU*. Final report. DOC: JTPF/002/2019/EN.

Forstater, M. (2017). Inditex, the limits of CbC data, and the meaning of 'aggressive avoidance'. *Tax Notes International, 85*(6), 565–569.

Forstater, M. (2018, May 2018). Why illicit financial flows and multinational tax avoidance are not the same thing. In *The Blog of International Centre for Tax and Development, ICTD*. Accessed May 22, 2019, from https://www.ictd.ac/blog/why-illicit-financial-flows-and-multinational-tax-avoidance-are-not-the-same-thing/

Freestone, T. (2018, Spring). Myth-busting the demise of commercial property insurance. In *InsuranceERM*.

Goldscheider, R. (2011). The classic 25% rule and the art of intellectual property licensing. *Duke Law and Technology Review, 6*, 1–22.

Hanken, J. et al. (2017). *Verrechnungspreise*, p. 483.

HMRC. International manual, INTM500000 https://www.gov.uk/hmrcinternal-manuals/international-manual/intm500000.

OECD. (2017a). OECD—Transfer pricing guidelines for multinational enterprises and tax administrations.

OECD. (2017b). OECD public discussion draft on "BEPS actions 8–10, financial transaction", 3rd July to 7th September 2017.

Osterwalder, A., & Pigneur, Y. (2010). *Business model generation*. Hoboken, NJ: Wiley.

Sanchez, D. (2011). *Mises on marginalism*. Accessed May 22, 2019, from https://mises.org/library/mises-marginalism

O. Treidler, *Transfer Pricing in One Lesson*, Management for Professionals,
https://doi.org/10.1007/978-3-030-25085-0

Standard & Poor. (2013, November 19). *Group rating methodology*. S&P Publication.
Treidler, O. (2017). Entrepreneurial transfer pricing—Embracing the arm's length principle. *Cayman Financial Review*, 3rd Quarter (48), 48–49.
Treidler, O. (2019). The rotten smell of the European tax agenda in 2019. *Cayman Financial Review*, 1st Quarter, (54).
Vögele, A. et al. (2015). Verrechnungspreise—4. Auflage, Chapter O, RN 627ff.
Worstall, T. (2018, July 19). Burberry destroys £28.6 million in stock—Why not, the stock is cheap, it's the brand that's valuable. Accessed May 22, 2019, from https://continentaltelegraph.com/business/burberry-destroys-28-6-million-in-stock-why-not-the-stock-is-cheap-its-the-brand-thats-valuable/

Printed in Great Britain
by Amazon

67755903R00085